W9-ADF-757

Ancient Peoples and Places

NUBIA UNDER THE PHARAOHS

General Editor

PROFESSOR GLYN DANIEL

ABOUT THE AUTHOR

Born in Cambridge, Ontario, Bruce Trigger took a B.A. *in honours anthropology at the University of Toronto and a doctorate in anthropology at Yale University in 1964. He taught at Northwestern University before moving to McGill University, Montreal, where he is now Professor of Anthropology. He has been the chairman of the Department of Anthropology at that University since 1970.*

Dr Trigger has excavated in Egypt and the Sudan and has published numerous studies related to that area and to the ethnohistory of eastern Canada. He has also published on the history and methodology of prehistoric archaeology.

Among his previous published books are History and Settlement in Lower Nubia *(1965),* Beyond History: The Methods of Prehistory *(1968) and* The Huron: Farmers of the North *(1969).*

NUBIA
UNDER THE
PHARAOHS

Bruce G. Trigger

74 PHOTOGRAPHS
43 LINE DRAWINGS
10 MAPS

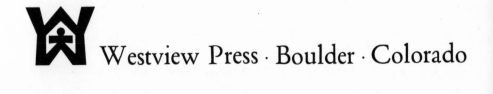

Westview Press · Boulder · Colorado

THIS IS VOLUME EIGHTY-FIVE IN THE SERIES
Ancient Peoples and Places
GENERAL EDITOR: PROFESSOR GLYN DANIEL

Library of Congress Cataloging in Publication Data

Trigger, Bruce G.
    Nubia under the pharaohs.
    (Ancient peoples and places; v. 85)
    Bibliography: p.
    Includes index.
    1. Nubia—History.   I. Title.
DT135.N8T74   1976   932'.01   76-168
ISBN 0-89158-544-3

Filmset by Keyspools Limited, Golborne, Lancashire, and printed in
Great Britain by Camelot Press Ltd., Southampton.

CONTENTS

List of Illustrations

Three intensive campaigns connected with successive dam-building projects near Aswan have made Lower Nubia archaeologically one of the best known regions of Africa. While earlier work was preoccupied with the impact that dynastic Egypt had upon Nubia, the most recent archaeological campaign, associated with the construction of the High Dam, has resulted in a growing awareness of the significant continuities in Nubian development from Palaeolithic times to the present. In this book, I seek to draw upon both themes and propose to treat Nubia as a case study of the social, economic, and cultural development of the adjacent hinterland of an ancient civilization. *Nubia Under the Pharaohs* might have been subtitled: the archaeology of an ancient imperialism.

In the absence of a standard system for transcribing ancient Egyptian proper names or Arabic place names into the Latin alphabet, I have opted in favour of individual transcriptions that are simple and familiar. I make no pretence of scientific rigour; such uniformity as has been achieved is solely as a matter of convenience.

I wish to thank my colleagues William Y. Adams, David O'Connor, and William K. Simpson for offering their detailed comments on the first draft of the book and K. Michalowski, T. Säve-Söderbergh and Peter Shinnie for clarifying a number of specific queries.

Apart from institutions, I wish to acknowledge the generous assistance of the following individuals who helped me to assemble the photographs that appear in this volume: William Y. Adams, Edward Brovarski, Mary Crawford, Michela Schiff Giorgini, Labib Habachi, Friedrich Hinkel, Fritz and Ursula Hintze, George R. Hughes, Ruth T. Marcanti, Hans-Åke Nordström, David O'Connor, Karl-Heinz Priese, Torgny Säve-Söderbergh, William K. Simpson, Harry S. Smith, and Jean Vercoutter. The figures have been redrawn by Stuart Munro-Hay, and the manuscript was typed by Jeanette Fernandez.

I also wish to record my special gratitude to Professor William K. Simpson. Under his direction I did my first fieldwork in Nubia and he has generously continued to support and encourage my Nubian studies in many ways.

Finally, it is appropriate that I dedicate this book to my father, John W. Trigger. It was he who, in the midst of a trying illness, found time to infect his seven-year-old son with a now clearly incurable fascination for ancient Egypt.   B.G.T.

CHAPTER I

The Archaeology of Nubia

THE ARCHAEOLOGY OF EMPIRE

As the first civilizations evolved, their rulers frequently sought to extend their influence over neighbouring less developed lands and peoples. Such activities took many forms and often led to the outright annexation of these peripheral regions. Motives included securing safe boundaries for established states; protecting trade routes; and exploiting the natural resources and human populations of these areas. Conquest also yielded immediate returns in the form of booty to enhance the prestige of the victorious ruler. The exploitation of these regions was especially important because many of the zones of fertile, easily worked soils that supported the earliest civilizations were poor in wood, copper, ivory, animal pelts, and other natural products that these civilizations de-pended upon or valued highly. By contrast, the adjacent, thinly populated deserts, mountains, and steppes were often rich in such items.

Occasionally, conquered territories provided outlets for the expanding population of the dominant power. While the settlement of conquered territory is often labelled colonialism and distinguished from imperialism, or the occupation of foreign lands solely for economic exploitation, this distinction may not be of great importance for understanding Egyptian activities in Nubia. Imperial expansion frequently compelled the inhabitants of peripheral areas to seek refuge in more distant localities and resulted in large numbers of people being carried off as slaves or forcibly resettled nearer the centre of empires. Those who remained behind were incorporated to varying degrees within the administrative frameworks of ancient civilizations through the imposition of censuses, corvees, and taxes, coercive social control, and centrally directed projects of economic exploitation.

Such controls were rarely imposed consistently or in a simple cumula-tive fashion over a long period of time. The personalities of monarchs and the domestic political circumstances in which they found themselves played no small part in determining the extent of their imperial ambitions. Moreover, the dynastic governments of pre-industrial civilizations

underwent cyclical phases of expansion and decline, as first studied in
detail by the medieval Arab historian Ibn Khaldun.¹ The growing
ineptitude of the central government meant that its control of outlying
regions weakened or lapsed altogether, only to be reaffirmed (perhaps
in a new fashion) when a strong new dynasty emerged. Periods of weak-
ness also provided opportunities for peripheral regions to become
nascent centres of political power vying for control of the civilization's
heartland.

This early imperialism resembles in many ways that of more recent
times. Yet, until we learn more about the imperial policies of pre-
industrial societies, it is difficult to ascertain to what degree these
resemblances are significant and to what degree they are superficial.
Because such imperialism played an important role in the spread of
civilization, an understanding of its earliest manifestations is also a
matter of considerable historical importance. Fortunately, this is an
area of study in which archaeological data can be of value.²

GEOLOGY AND TOPOGRAPHY

Fig. 1

Nubia is generally defined as the portion of the Nile Valley that lies
between Aswan, which was the southern border of Egypt in Pharaonic
times, and the Khartoum district; however, at present the Nubian
languages are no longer spoken above the Fourth Cataract which lies
close to the southern limits of effective Egyptian control during New
Kingdom times. We are therefore little concerned with the region to the
south.

Because it lies directly up the Nile River from Egypt, Nubia is ideally
located for studying the colonial activities of one of the earliest and most
long lived civilizations of antiquity. Having very limited agricultural
potential, Nubia has not experienced the dramatic population explosion
that, since the beginning of the nineteenth century, has erased so many
records of the past from the Nile Valley north of Aswan. Nor have
ancient sites been buried under accumulating silt as they have been to
the north. It has therefore been possible to obtain a fairly accurate
picture of the nature and distribution of sites over many thousands of
years. The farsighted archaeological projects that have been associated
with dam-building at Aswan throughout the twentieth century have
led to more archaeological data being collected concerning the northern

Fig. 1 General map of Nubia >

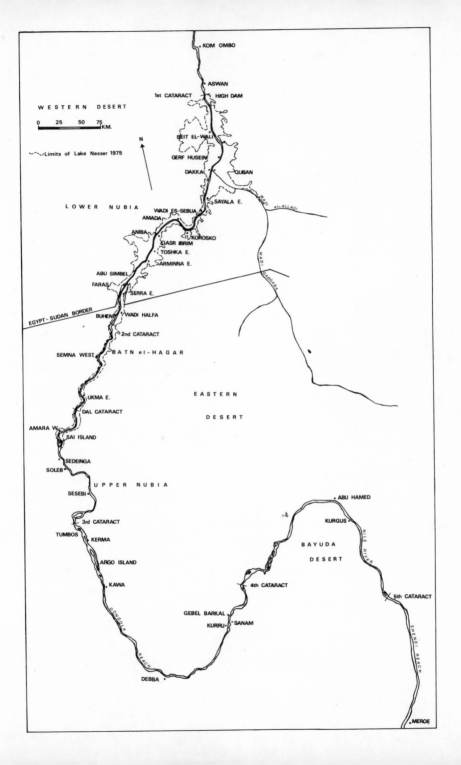

KOM OMBO

ASWAN
1st CATARACT   HIGH DAM

WESTERN   DESERT

0   25   50   75
                KM.

BEIT EL-WALI

Limits of Lake Nasser 1975

GERF HUSEIN

N

DAKKA   QUBAN

LOWER   NUBIA   WADI ES-SEBUA

SAYALA E.

AMADA

ANIBA

KOROSKO

QASR IBRIM

TOSHKA E.

ARMINNA E.

ABU SIMBEL

FARAS

SERRA E.

EGYPT - SUDAN BORDER

BUHEN   WADI HALFA

2nd CATARACT

SEMNA WEST   BATN el-HAGAR

EASTERN

DESERT

UKMA E.

DAL CATARACT

AMARA W.

SAI ISLAND

SEDEINGA

SOLEB

UPPER   NUBIA

SESEBI

3rd CATARACT

TUMBOS   KERMA

ARGO ISLAND

KAWA

4th CATARACT

GEBEL BARKAL

KURRU   SANAM

DEBBA

ABU HAMED

KURGUS

BAYUDA

DESERT

5th CATARACT

MEROE

WADI el-ALLAQI

WADI GABGABA

NILE RIVER

DONGOLA REACH

SHENDI REACH

part of Nubia than are available for any comparable part of Africa.

Nubia is located in the centre of the hottest and most arid region of the world. As far south as Dongola, groundwater and vegetation are limited to the intermittent run-off that flows down the wadis from the Red Sea Hills and to the small oases of the Western Desert. Throughout Nubia, as in Egypt, sedentary life depends wholly on the Nile and largely on water supplied by the annual inundation. North of Gebel es-Silsila, in southern Egypt, the river has cut a broad swath through Eocene limestone to create a floodplain up to 25 kilometres wide. Farther south the Nile has sliced more easily through Nubian sandstone to form a narrower and often discontinuous floodplain that is rarely more than 2 kilometres wide. For Egypt, the Nile is an unbroken artery of communication. Beginning at Aswan, however, is the first of a series of cataracts produced wherever the river is forced to cut across resistent igneous and metamorphic rock. These hindrances to travel divide the river into reaches of varying productivity.[3]

The northernmost reach, now completely flooded by the waters of the High Dam, lay between the First and Second Cataracts, the latter just south of Wadi Halfa. Fertile patches tended to be discontinuous and varied from small plots at the mouths of wadis to floodplains several kilometres long and up to 1.5 kilometres wide. These fertile patches were separated by areas where rocks and sand reached the river's edge. Archaeological sites of all periods clustered around these fertile patches, although they constituted only a small percentage of the land bordering the river. The richest areas in Lower Nubia were the Plain of Dakka, opposite the Wadi el-Allaqi, the Derr-Toshka region, centering on the recent provincial capital of Aniba, and the region south of Abu Simbel, centering on Faras. The landscape adjacent to the Nile is highly variable in Lower Nubia. In some areas sand and gravel deposits rise gently to the adjacent plateau; elsewhere the less complete dissection of the plateau has left a hilly landscape reaching to the edge of the river.

Between the Second and Dal Cataracts, the river makes its way through a region of igneous and metamorphic rock known as the Batn el-Hagar or 'Belly of Rocks'. In this region the channel is often broken and unsuitable for navigation in the dry season, while travel along the banks of the river is difficult in many places. Alluvial patches are smaller and more infrequent than they are farther north, but small villages are found wherever there is farmland. South of the Batn el-Hagar, these areas of fertile soil again become larger and more frequent.

In the Dongola Reach, between the Third and Fourth Cataracts, the Nile flows in a single channel through a sandstone terrain. Below Debba, the fertile terraces are continuous but relatively narrow and at Letti and Kerma there are large natural basins: low lying areas of alluvium in which the floodwaters can be held until the ground is sufficiently wetted to produce crops. In the upper part of the reach where the river flows southwest for almost 300 kilometres before resuming its northerly course, extensive silt and sand-covered banks are revealed at low water, while terraces of fossil silts are flooded in years of exceptionally high Niles. Hence in this region there can be great variation in the amount of arable land from one year to the next. Beyond these terraces the land rises gently to sand or gravel covered plains which are interrupted by only a few hills.

Between the Fourth and Fifth Cataracts is one of the least populated or hospitable sections of the Nile. A narrow trench has been incised into igneous and metamorphic rock in such a way as to leave few terraces of alluvial soil. Below Abu Hamed, the prevailing northeast winds blow in the same direction as the river current, making navigation upstream difficult. In antiquity, the preferred line of communication between the Dongola and Shendi Reaches ran overland across the Bayuda Desert.

RESOURCES

Nubian farmers have traditionally grown wheat, barley, and millet, and a variety of fruits and vegetables. Floodplain agriculture produces only one crop a year, which grows during the winter. The use of the *shaduf* (a hand-operated water hoist) and the *saqiya* (an oxen-driven waterwheel), neither of which was known in early antiquity, permits crops to be grown above the high water level and hence throughout the year. Irrigated land is often intensively cultivated. Basin agriculture is limited to the region north of Aswan and to parts of Dongola. Animal husbandry is only slightly less important than growing crops. Animals have traditionally grazed on the wild grasses and stubble of the floodplain during most of the year so that fodder was required only during the flood season. The date palm has grown profusely in Nubia since early times. In the past, Nubian dates were prized for their excellent quality and were exported to Egypt in large numbers, making them the principal cash crop of the region.

Prior to the building of the High Dam, the population of the Nile Valley between the First and Fourth Cataracts was over 400,000. It appears that this population had not significantly increased since the early nineteenth century, whereas the population of Egypt, supported by an expanding irrigation system such as could not exist in Nubia, rose from two and a half million to thirty million. Thus modern figures may be misleading. In Pharaonic times, Nubia may have had a population one-tenth as large as the four million estimated for Egypt.[4]

The deserts immediately adjacent to Lower Nubia lack all plant and animal life and are largely uninhabited by humans. Nearer the river there are rabbits and gazelles as well as hyenas, whose reputed ferocity is much feared by the Nubians. An occasional crocodile was still reported north of Abu Simbel as late as 1960 and in the last century they were common throughout Nubia. Birds are plentiful along the river and cobras, horned vipers, and scorpions require people to be careful. Beja herdsmen from the Red Sea Hills wintered along the Nile in Lower Nubia, while in the Merowe region members of the Shaiqiya tribes still alternate between the south bank of the river and the thin pastures of the Bayuda Desert. Nomadism is, however, less important in this area than in the monsoon belt farther south.

The accumulation of wind-driven sand poses a threat to fields and villages alike in many districts along the west bank of the Nile. While the deserts today produce little that is of value, gold mining was formerly of considerable importance in the Eastern Desert, particularly in the upper portions of the Wadi el-Allaqi. Diorite and semi-precious stones were mined by the ancient Egyptians on both sides of the Nile and acacia trees, which grew in the wadi bottoms, were cut for timber and charcoal.

Prior to the introduction of the camel in Ptolemaic times and the later development of the Saharan caravan trade, the Nile corridor was one of the main routes by which slaves as well as ivory, ebony, skins, and other products of sub-Saharan Africa could be transported north to the Mediterranean. Thus from an economic point of view Nubia was a region of considerable importance. Yet by comparison with Egypt the whole of Nubia was poor and capable of supporting only a dispersed population. Many aspects of Nubia's role as a colonial hinterland may be attributed to this contradiction.

European travellers began to penetrate south of Aswan in 1813. The first comprehensive description of the region, including its antiquities, is the report of John Lewis Burckhardt's journey by camel between Aswan and the Dongola Reach. In 1817, Giovanni Belzoni, the circus strong man turned collector of antiquities, was able to clear away enough sand to enter the Great Temple at Abu Simbel. In 1819, Jean-Nicolas Huyot sketched sites and recorded inscriptions in Nubia and some of his work played an important role in Jean-François Champollion's decipherment of Egyptian hieroglyphs. François-Chrétien Gau's visit of the same year formed the basis for his *Antiquités de la Nubie*, the first publication to deal specifically with Nubian archaeology. Between 1842 and 1845, a Prussian expedition led by Karl Richard Lepsius systematically copied and published the monuments of Egypt and Nubia, thereby preserving a record of many inscriptions that are now either destroyed or badly mutilated. From 1905 to 1907, James Breasted undertook to photograph and copy all Egyptian historical texts from Nubia and in 1907 Wallis Budge published *The Egyptian Sudan*, a monumental work based on all literary sources known at that time.[5]

By the end of the nineteenth century, the desire for an increased water supply to grow two or three crops a year instead of the one traditionally grown throughout Egypt had resulted in the construction of a series of dams throughout Egypt. The largest of these was the first Aswan Dam, built at Shellal between 1899 and 1902. It was 130 feet high and when full flooded the valley as far south as Wadi es-Sebua. The only archaeological work carried out in connection with this project was to survey and strengthen the temple of Philae, which dates mainly from Ptolemaic-Roman times. In 1906, Arthur Weigall made a brief archaeological survey of Lower Nubia, recording important data about temples, rock inscriptions, and the location of cemeteries.

In 1907, it was decided to heighten the Aswan Dam by $16\frac{1}{2}$ feet and this time funds were set aside for a thorough archaeological examination of the northern half of Egyptian Nubia. Two projects were under⁓ taken. The first was concerned with the consolidation and recording of major historical monuments. It was placed under the Department of Antiquities and its results were published in a 15⁓volume series, *Les temples immergés de la Nubie*. The second project, under the direction of the Survey Department, was to find and record cemeteries and other archaeological sites that were located up to the 115 metre contour line, the highest point to be affected by raising the dam. Both banks of the river were to be traversed in order to locate as many sites as possible; every important site was to be completely excavated; and less important ones were to be sampled and their outlines traced. Both artefacts and human skeletal remains were to be studied. George A. Reisner, who was put in charge of the survey, established systematic methods for recording finds. These included mapping and recording each grave on a separate 'tomb card'. His system, which was the earliest programme of extensive salvage archaeology, produced a clear record of the work which the survey accomplished and set a standard for subsequent work in Nubia and elsewhere.

During the first season (1907–8), fifty cemeteries and a few habitation sites were investigated over a 50 kilometre stretch of river.[6] The results permitted Reisner to construct a cultural sequence based on units that could be correlated with periods of Egyptian history. A local culture called the 'A⁓Group' was matched with the Early Dynastic period. This was seen as a continuation of Predynastic cultures historically linked to those of Upper Egypt. The next phase, now known to be spurious, was called the 'B⁓Group' and was correlated with the Old Kingdom. A 'C⁓Group' was made coeval with the First Intermediate Period and the Middle Kingdom and was followed by a 'D⁓Group' indistinguishable from New Kingdom material in Egypt proper. There was little evidence of any occupation of Lower Nubia between the end of the New King⁓ dom and the Ptolemaic period. A sequence of cultures was worked out for later times but is not relevant to the present study. From 1908 to 1911, under the direction of C. M. Firth, the survey was extended as far south as Wadi es⁓Sebua; confirming and refining Reisner's sequence.[7] Aside from some rather superficial work in the Middle Kingdom forts at Ikkur and Quban, the main effort was directed towards the examination of about 150 cemeteries. A number of Pharaonic town⁓

sites had been noted by earlier travellers, but most of these had been flooded by the construction of the first dam.

During the same period, several other expeditions were working outside the survey area. Between 1907 and 1910, the Eckley B. Coxe Expedition of the University of Pennsylvania, led by C. L. Woolley and D. Randall-MacIver, excavated a C-Group settlement at Amada and around the Egyptian settlements at Aniba and Buhen. Between 1910 and 1912, the Oxford Expedition led by F. L. Griffith worked at Faras West, finding sites from every period of Nubian history. Afterwards they excavated for a season at the early Kushite cemetery of Sanam, near the Fourth Cataract. At Aniba, the large Egyptian fort and cemeteries of the Middle and New Kingdoms as well as Nubian material were excavated by the Ernst von Sieglin Expedition between 1912 and 1914 and again between 1929 and 1933. Between 1910 and 1912, the Austrian Egyptologist Hermann Junker excavated an A-Group and a C-Group cemetery at Kubanieh, just north of Aswan, and C-Group cemeteries at Arminna East and Toshka West. At the latter site he was able to demonstrate that the C-Group had lasted well into the Second Intermediate Period.[8]

Just before World War I, Reisner began to work in the Sudan. He carried out important excavations at what he believed were the remains of a Middle Kingdom Egyptian colony at Kerma, among the New Kingdom temples at Gebel Barkal (1912–16), and at Semna, Kumma, and other Middle Kingdom forts in the vicinity of the Second Cataract (1924–32). Although Reisner managed to write up only the report on his work at Kerma, the rest of his Sudan excavations have been published posthumously by Dows Dunham.

By World War I, archaeological work had ceased in Lower Nubia and it did not begin again until 1929. At that time a new project was astir to heighten the Aswan Dam to 122 metres above sea level, which would raise water levels through all of Egyptian Nubia. It was therefore decided to re-activate the Archaeological Survey of Nubia under the direction of Walter Emery. In 1929, he and L. P. Kirwan began to survey the sites along the west bank of the Nile between Wadi es-Sebua and the Sudanese border.[9] The following year, Emery and Kirwan discovered the great cemeteries at Qustul and Ballana near the Sudanese border. These cemeteries contained the graves of Nubian kings of the fourth to sixth centuries AD and their excavation took up the remaining three seasons that had been allotted to surveying the east bank of the Nile prior to flooding. Emery's work did little to alter or amplify previous interpretations of the history of Nubia in Pharaonic times.

Between 1929 and 1936, the Oxford Expedition excavated the New Kingdom settlement at Kawa, near the Third Cataract, while the Egypt Exploration Society excavated the towns of Sesebi in 1937 and Amara West between 1938 and 1950. In 1950, the Sudan Antiquities Service began a regular programme of excavations which in the course of the next decade involved work at Kor, Sai, Debeira, and Buhen. Since 1957, the University of Pisa has excavated each year at the Upper Nubian temple sites of Soleb and Sedeinga.

RECENT EXCAVATIONS

Interest in Nubian archaeology was intensified in 1959 when plans were announced for the construction of the High Dam at Aswan. The dam was to be 111 metres high and would flood the Nile Valley over 200 kilometres south of the Sudanese border. An appeal for archaeological work issued by Unesco met with enthusiastic international response. The most publicized work of this campaign was the detailed recording of all of the Egyptian temples in this area and the removal of many of them to places of safety. The largest of these removal projects was the transfer of the two temples at Abu Simbel on to the plateau above the flooded cliffs into which they had originally been cut. Less well known are the removal to new locations above high water level of the large Roman temple at Kalabsha and the New Kingdom temple at Amada; the transfer to Khartoum of the small temples at Buhen, Semna and Kumma; and the saving of many other minor Egyptian temples for re-erection in Egypt or abroad.

Equally important were the excavations that were carried out. In 1961 Harry Smith undertook to complete the archaeological survey of Egyptian Nubia in all areas not already assigned to other expeditions. His team located some fifty sites between the high-water level and the 180 metre contour line. In the Sudan, the Sudan Antiquities Service and the Scandinavian Joint Expedition undertook to survey south from the Egyptian border. Over forty expeditions from all parts of the world took up concessions to excavate sites or to examine specific stretches of river in Egypt and the Sudan. Among the most significant results of this work were the first detailed studies of the Palaeolithic archaeology of Lower Nubia and the elucidation of the chronology and culture history of Nubia from the sixth century AD to modern times; the latter being accomplished by William Y. Adams while working for Unesco and the Sudan Antiquities Service. Certain specific discoveries were of importance for the history of Pharaonic Nubia. Among these were the first A-Group buildings and the first superstructures covering A-Group graves to be identified in Nubia.[10] Emery excavated an Old Kingdom settlement at Buhen, which is the earliest unequivocal evidence of Egyptian settlement in Nubia.[11] He also carried out an important study of the military architecture at the fortress of Buhen, while Jean Vercoutter's meticulous excavations at Mirgissa yielded important information about the functioning of a major Middle Kingdom fort.[12] William K. Simpson's publication of the tomb of Hekanefer and Säve-Söderbergh's study of those of Djehutyhotep and Amenemhet have extended our knowledge of the Egyptianized Nubian elite of the New Kingdom.[13]

The work done in Nubia has also stimulated a valuable rethinking of major problems of Nubian culture history. Harry Smith has effectively disproved the separate existence of Reisner's B-Group;[14] Manfred Bietak and David O'Connor have re-analyzed the data concerning the C-Group and related cultures;[15] and Adams has raised disturbing questions about the chronology of New Kingdom sites and the nature of Egyptian-Nubian relations during this period.[16] Fritz Hintze, stimulated by Säve-Söderbergh's earlier work, has proposed a still more radical re-interpretation of Reisner's ideas about the Kerma culture.[17] There has also been a growing tendency to view Nubian history in a broader regional context and to stress ethnic and cultural continuities rather than discontinuities.

While further work is impossible on sites of the Pharaonic period in Lower Nubia (except Qasr Ibrim), archaeological excavations have barely scratched the surface farther south. Thus any study of Pharaonic Nubia is written with a northern bias and is subject to all of the limita-tions that this differential in our knowledge of the various parts of Nubia imposes on us.

The Archaeology of Nubia

EPIGRAPHIC SOURCES

Archaeological data constitute only one of two major sources of information about Pharaonic Nubia; the other is the written records of the ancient Egyptians. These two types of data are complementary. Archaeology provides a record of everyday life in Nubia amongst that country's native inhabitants and Egyptian conquerors. By contrast, written records inform us about the aspirations, policies, and propaganda of Nubia's real and aspiring Egyptian rulers. Unfortunately, written records are fragmentary and for the early historic period are almost non-existent. Deliberate destruction, chance preservation, and chance discovery all help to distort further the picture of Nubian history that is derived from these records. Such shortcomings are compounded by a still far from perfect understanding of the ancient Egyptian lexicon and by the brevity of the recorded accounts.

The monumental inscriptions expressed the power of a divine monarch whose existence ensured the proper functioning of an Egypt-centred world. As such, the texts are both egocentric and ethnocentric; battles of doubtful outcome are turned into personal victories for the king and marriage alliances with sovereigns of equal power are described as the payment of tribute to the Egyptian court.[18] Many a list of conquered provinces has turned out to be a copy of a centuries old text, its magical potency undiminished by changing political fortunes. Foreign lands and peoples named in Egyptian texts are frequently unknown to us and their status is further obscured by a lexicon that used the same terms for all foreign rulers, whether they were tribal headmen or the kings of powerful foreign countries. Likewise, a single word denoted tribute paid by conquered states, goodwill presents from independent states, and the proceeds of trade carried on with the Pharaoh's brother monarchs in southwestern Asia. Given the problems of both the archaeological and the epigraphic record it is not surprising that on some occasions they appear to contradict rather than to reinforce one another. Such contradictions must be assumed to be apparent rather than real and indicate serious gaps in our understanding of Nubian history or the behaviour of the ancient Egyptians. Among existing published works, the most important study of Nubian history based mainly on textual material is T. Säve-Söderbergh's *Agypten und Nubien*.[19]

CHAPTER II

Prehistory

It used to be believed that in prehistoric times the Nile Valley in Egypt and Nubia was a vast swampland similar to the present Sudd region of the Upper Nile. According to these theories, the transformation of the valley into arable land was the result of human effort. It has now been demonstrated that while the coastal regions of the Delta and the deepest parts of the floodplain formerly sustained perennial swamps and thickets, most of the plain was only seasonally inundated and in the winter and spring was covered with lush savanna-like vegetation that served as natural grazing land. While the Nile teemed with crocodile, hippopotamus, and fish, these adjacent plains supported large numbers of elephant, rhinoceros, ostrich, wild ass, and cattle, with antelope, gazelle, ibex, and deer living on the drier flanks. Increased rainfall periodically permitted vegetation and animal life to prosper in the adjacent deserts. There is evidence of periods of increased runoff since the last ice age; particularly between 9200 and 6000 BC and again after 5000 BC. Following a dry interval before 4000 BC there was another wet period, with fairly abundant vegetation flourishing in the wadis of northern and eastern Egypt until *c.* 2350 BC.[1]

Plate 1

Beginning at least 50,000 years ago, the Nile went through a number of cycles of greater discharge which in Nubia laid down a series of flood plains up to 42 metres higher than the present one. These cycles of aggradation appear to correlate with locally higher rainfall, suggesting that the main pluvial trends north and south of the Sahara were in phase. In the intervals, there were cycles of downcutting when wind-blown sands encroached on the former floodplain. These cycles of aggradation and downcutting considerably altered the width of the floodplain and its capacity to support plant and animal life. At all times, however, the Nile Valley in Nubia must have had a considerably lower carrying capacity and hence a more restricted capacity for cultural development than did the broader Nile Valley to the north, even though the flora and fauna were much the same in Nubia and Egypt.[2]

The shift of the Sudanese summer rainbelts northward during periods of greater precipitation probably produced considerable climatic amelioration in the desert areas adjacent to the Dongola Reach. The northern part of Nubia was the area least well placed to benefit from a southward expansion of the Mediterranean winter rains or a northward expansion of Sudanese summer rainfall. Butzer and Hansen maintain that even in relatively favourable Late Palaeolithic times (15,000–10,000 BC) a savanna-like environment was confined to the Nile floodplain and to wadi bottoms. At this period, hartebeest, gazelle, Barbary sheep, and wild asses favoured the wadis, while wild cattle and other large game frequented the floodplain.[3]

LATE PALAEOLITHIC CULTURES

Egypt and Nubia were long held to be culturally backward areas during the Late Palaeolithic period. Recent excavations in Upper Egypt and Nubia have shown this view to be false; these areas were participating fully in the technological advances that were occurring in adjacent parts of Africa and Eurasia.[4] According to Wendorf, the beginning of the Nubian Late Palaeolithic is approximately coeval with the Masmas Aggradation (22,000–16,000 BC). Most Late Palaeolithic sites are small seasonal camps located near prehistoric Nile channels. Subsistence was derived principally from hunting large savanna-type mammals and from fishing.[5] The mosaic of Late Palaeolithic industries now being found in Upper Egypt and Nubia may result from diverse populations being thrown into closer juxtaposition as a consequence of desiccation or from an expansion of population, producing numerous micro-adaptations within the framework of a hunting and gathering economy. The Sebekian site at Kom Ombo suggests that as early as 12,000 BC abundant natural resources were being exploited intensively, permitting bands to inhabit single encampments throughout the year by feeding off riverine resources, migratory birds, and various animals as they became available.[6] J. D. Clark has interpreted the large number of individuals who had met violent deaths from the cemetery at Gebel Sahaba in Lower Nubia (*c.* 12,000 BC) as evidence of warfare resulting from serious population pressure at this time.[7] The skeletons from this cemetery are said to resemble the Cro-Magnon type, especially of the North African Mechta variety.[8]

Fig. 2

*Fig. 2 Late Palaeolithic cultural sequences in Egypt and Nubia (25,000 to 3,000 BC) >
(after Clark 1971, fig. 2 and Wendorf 1968: 1042)*

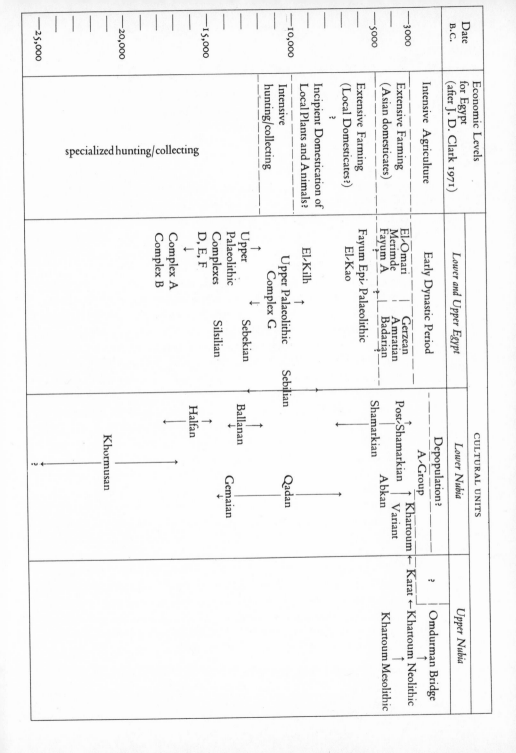

The earliest Late Palaeolithic culture to be defined in Nubia is the Khormusan, which lasted from about 25,000 to 16,000 BC. It is characterized by an evolved Levallois technique and by large numbers of unretouched Levallois flakes, denticulates and burins; the latter probably used to work wood and reeds. An increasing number of tools were manufactured from Nile chert, the main type of stone employed by later industries. The use of burins and the abandonment of the ferrocrete sandstone of the desert plateaus are additional features pointing to an adjustment to a specifically Nilotic environment.

The final phases of the Khormusan culture appear to be contemporary with the Halfan and Gemaian cultures. The Halfan is estimated to have lasted from 18,000 to 15,000 BC and exhibits a transition from a microflake to a true microblade industry. It and the coeval Khor es-Sil II and III industry at Kom Ombo indicate a microblade technology along the Nile much earlier than elsewhere in Africa. The earliest Gemaian sites in Lower Nubia date from about the time the Halfan culture disappears, but the low frequency of blade tools in Gemaian seems to rule out the possibility of a developmental link between Halfan and Gemaian. In Gemaian, as in Khormusan, the Levallois element is significant and burins and denticulates are also important. Shiner believes that the Gemaian culture gave rise to the Qadan and Abkan cultures. The Qadan culture (? 13,000–4000 BC) is a microlithic industry made on tiny radially prepared flakes and cores. In its later stages blades outnumber flakes. Wendorf tentatively attributes part of this increase to the influence of the Ballanan industry, which appeared about 14,000 BC and flourished briefly in Lower Nubia. The most common tools are truncated microblades struck from single and opposed platform cores made of Nile chert. The Ballanan seems intrusive and may be related to a blade industry known for Upper Egypt.

The most interesting of the Qadan sites is No. 8905 from Toshka West, which dates c. 12,500 BC. Large numbers of grinding stones were found in that site as well as a few lustrous-edged lunates apparently used to cut grass or a similar flexible substance containing silica. An analysis of microflora trapped in associated tufa revealed smut fungus as well as gramineae pollen and tissue from an unidentified grass. This suggests that some grass, possibly barley, was being harvested at that site. Wendorf does not conclude that it was a domestic variety, but suggests that here we may have evidence of a first step towards plant domestication.[9] The earliest grinding stones yet known come from the Khor es-Sil II site in the Kom Ombo area which is dated *c.* 15,000 BC. Other grindstones from Kom Ombo and farther north date between 15,000 and 9000 BC. The evidence thus suggests that between 15,000 and 9000 BC the inhabitants of this region were making significant use of wild grain and seeds along with other plant and animal resources.[10]

There is no evidence that the use of grain persisted or gave rise to food production in Nubia or Upper Egypt. Grindstones occur only sporadic-ally in the later Stone Age cultures and there is no increase in the size of settlements in Lower Nubia before the fourth millennium BC. Wendorf argues that increasing desiccation sometime after 10,000 BC may have curtailed the wild grains on which an intensive collecting economy was based.[11] If so, we must assume that, contrary to Clark's argument, the pressure on food resources was not sufficient to encourage the domestica-tion of grain as wild varieties began to diminish in quantity.

Fishing appears to have played an important role in the Qadan and other Late Palaeolithic cultures of Nubia. Large numbers of mud fish (*Clarias*) were eviscerated and smoked at site No. 8905, while at Cat Fish Cave, near Korosko, a stratum dated *c.* 6500 BC was found to contain numerous remains of mud fish as well as 38 bone harpoons resembling those from the possibly contemporary Khartoum Mesolithic culture farther south.[12]

Other cultures occur in Lower Nubia for the Late Palaeolithic. The Sebilian sites are dated *c.* 13,000 to 9000 BC and resemble the Lower Sebilian ones from Kom Ombo. This culture is markedly different from contemporary ones in Lower Nubia. One archaic feature is the use of ferrocrete to make tools, which may explain the crude aspect of the industry as a whole. It is suggested that the Sebilian may represent the intrusion of a Tshitolian related culture from central Africa. This challenges the traditional view that the Sebilian developed from the Middle Palaeolithic tradition of southern Egypt.[13] The final industries to be defined are the Arkinian (*c.* 7500 BC) and the Shamarkian (5750–4500 BC). These are known from only one location on the west bank of the Nile near Wadi Halfa and a Saharan origin has been suggested for both of them. On the other hand, these cultures also share features with the earlier Halfan and Ballanan cultures.[14]

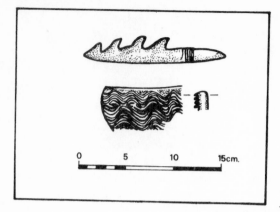

Fig. 3 Khartoum Mesolithic artefacts. Above, bone harpoon; below, pottery fragment (after Arkell 1949)

Fig. 3

Evidence of increasing sedentariness along the southern fringes of the Sahara in Holocene times is provided by the apparently pre-agricultural 'Khartoum Mesolithic' culture, whose type site at Khartoum appears to have been inhabited at least seasonally for a long period of time.[15] A wide variety of animal bones was found, as well as bone harpoons and grinding stones; although Arkell believes that the latter were used only for grinding ochre. The apparently negroid inhabitants of the site also gathered the fruit of wild trees such as *Celtis integrifolia*. Excavations here and at the Shabona site to the south of Khartoum suggest a collecting economy based on a wide range of plants and animals.[16]

Shelters were constructed of reeds covered with clay and conical brown pottery bowls were decorated with wavy lines and later also with dots. The pottery appears to be indigenous to this part of Africa. Related forms have been found as far north as Dongola and from Kassala in the east to Ennedi, Ténéré, and Ahaggar in the west. Some of the latter has been radiocarbon dated between 6000 and 5000 BC. This type of pottery is associated with different lithic traditions and seems to have been widespread among established local groups. Its broad distribution probably bears witness to the growing sedentariness made possible by the highly successful collecting economy that flourished along the southern fringes of the Sahara during a period of greater rainfall in the fourth millennium or earlier.[17]

Between 8000 and 5000 BC the floodplain north of Aswan was lower than it is today and the valley narrower; as a result most archaeological sites from this period are now buried and inaccessible.[18] It nevertheless appears that whatever domestication of plants and animals was going on at this time in the Nile Valley or the adjacent deserts played only a minor role in the development of the Predynastic cultures of the Delta and Upper Egypt. The subsistence economies of these societies were based on the same complex of domesticated plants (wheat, barley, flax) and animals (cattle, pig, sheep, goats) that was already established in adjacent parts of southwestern Asia. There is no evidence that the wild ancestors of sheep and goats ever lived in Africa and the essential similarity of the Egyptian and southwest Asian subsistence patterns suggests that even if some Egyptian plants and animals were domesticated locally this was the result of specific ideas about domestication that were of southwest Asian origin. The only local domesticate of lasting importance (except for the cat which was domesticated in historic times) was the donkey. Whatever uniquely African plants and animals may have been domesticated in earlier times gave way before the superior kinds of domesticates that had been developed in southwestern Asia.[19]

The oldest direct evidence of food production south of Aswan comes from the Khartoum Neolithic culture whose type site, Shaheinab, is located on the west bank of the Nile about 50 kilometres north of Khartoum. This site has been radiocarbon dated 3500 to 3100 BC, which is coeval with radiocarbon dates for the Gerzean culture of Upper Egypt. This culture, unlike the Khartoum Mesolithic, appears to have been confined to the Nile Valley and to locally adjacent steppe land. The brown pottery cooking vessels, which were up to 45 centimetres in diameter and now generally burnished, were decorated with shallow punctate patterns usually made using fragments of mussel shell. The rims of pots tended to be elaborately decorated. This brown ware had clearly developed from pottery of Khartoum Mesolithic type. In addition, there were new wares including black pottery and brown bowls with black rims and interiors. Stone celts suggest a new emphasis on woodworking, while the large numbers of mussel shells at Shaheinab indicate more utilization of riverine resources than in earlier times. There is also evidence that a wide range of animals, including giraffe,

Fig. 4

Prehistory

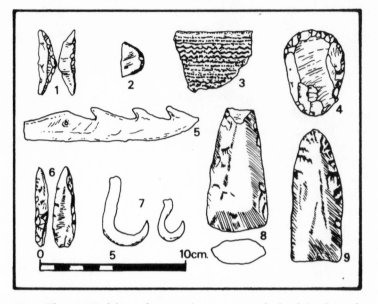

Fig. 4 Khartoum Neolithic artefacts: 1, 2 deep crescents; 3 sherd with dotted wavy line decoration; 4 end scraper; 5 bone harpoon; 6 drill; 7 fishhooks; 8 polished stone celt; 9 gouge (after Arkell 1953 and Clark 1970: fig. 59)

was being hunted. Significantly, however, two percent of the bones from the site were of sheep and goats.[20] Both are domesticates that are ultimately of southwest Asian origin. It is likely that these domesticates and perhaps the black-topped pottery had reached this part of the Sudan from Egypt and been adopted by the local population. Goats appear prior to domestic cattle at the Haua Fteah site in Cyrenaica (c. 4800 BC); which suggests that sheep and goats may have been adopted as domestic animals prior to cattle over much of northeastern Africa. No domesticated plants have yet been associated with the Khartoum Neolithic. Clark argues, however, that grindstones indicate that grasses were a major part of subsistence for both the Khartoum Mesolithic and the Khartoum Neolithic cultures and he speculates that a Khartoum Neolithic-type site dating between the fourth and second millennium BC may eventually produce the earliest evidence for the cultivation of sorghum.[21] Perhaps the quickening pace of desiccation at the end of the Neolithic Wet Phase stimulated a shift towards food production in this area.

Pottery resembling that of the Khartoum Neolithic has been found in sites in the Dongola region (the Karat Group) and also in the southern part of Lower Nubia (the Khartoum Variant culture). Yet the lithic material associated with the pottery in each of these areas differs greatly, suggesting the diffusion of a Khartoum Neolithic type of pottery among established groups living over a wide area. Although no direct evidence of food production has been obtained for the two northern cultures, the predominance of small sites in the Khartoum Variant both along the river and for 20 kilometres into the Western Desert has not unreasonably been interpreted as evidence of a pastoral economy. All of these sites are tentatively dated to the end of the fourth millennium.[22]

The oldest sites in Lower Nubia known to contain pottery belong to the Shamarkian culture and have been dated *c.* 4500 to 4000 BC. These sites, however, contain only minute amounts of pottery. Later 'Post-Shamarkian' sites in the same area are much larger and also contain pottery. On these grounds it has been suggested that they might have had 'neolithic' (food-producing) economies; however, there is no direct evidence of farming or herding. The Post-Shamarkian sites contain considerable amounts of imported Egyptian flint, indicating exchange with the north unattested for earlier times. These sites have been dated between *c.* 4600 and 3100 radiocarbon years BC.[23]

Another culture that may have been food-producing is the Abkan, which occurs along both banks of the Nile in the vicinity of the Second Cataract and possibly as far south as Ukma. The lithic industry associated with this culture appears to have developed from the Terminal Qadan culture. Abkan pottery occurs as plain, reddish-brown, open bowls. Multiple occupation sites cover sizable areas, which like the Post-Shamarkian ones suggest an expanding population. Hunting appears to have been of little importance although positive evidence about subsistence was not obtained. The presence of small numbers of Khartoum Variant sherds in Abkan sites and of Abkan sherds in Khartoum Variant sites indicates that these two cultures were at least partly contemporary.[24] It is unclear to what degree Abkan pottery is related to the pottery of the prehistoric Tergis and El Melik cultures of the Dongola area. The latter is red slipped with decoration restricted to a few incised lines.[25] Further investigation may also clarify if there is any historical connection between Abkan pottery and that of Predynastic Lower Egypt. It is not impossible that prior to the beginning of the Badarian culture in Upper Egypt a plain red pottery was manu⁄factured from the Delta south into Nubia.

THE A⁄GROUP

The beginnings of the A⁄Group culture in northern Lower Nubia were contemporary with the Abkan culture to the south. To account for the A⁄Group, however, it is necessary to understand the social and political transformation that took place in Egypt in the fourth millennium B C. At the beginning of the millennium, Upper Egypt was the home of the Amratian (Naqada I) culture which in spite of limited evidence of trade appears to have been a tribal society made up of many small self⁄sufficient groupings. By *c.* 3500 B C, however, at the beginning of the Gerzean (Naqada II) phase there is evidence of greater craft specializa⁄tion and the circulation of mass produced and luxury goods throughout Upper Egypt; more contact and trade with southwestern Asia; and an increasingly stratified society. Major centres such as This, Naqada, and Hierakonpolis appear to have become the nuclei of small states that were ruled over by petty kings, endowed with patron deities, and striving to control the lucrative Upper Egyptian gold trade with southwestern Asia.[26] By the end of the Gerzean period, conquest and alliances had united the whole Nile Valley north of Aswan under the leadership of the Thinite royal house.

Apart from the large amounts of imported Egyptian flint in the Post⁄Shamarkian culture there is no evidence that the slowly⁄developing and self⁄sufficient Badarian and Amratian societies exerted any significant influence in Lower Nubia. The earliest A⁄Group site in Lower Nubia is a cemetery at Khor Bahan, just south of Shellal. This cemetery appears to have been used by a small community that cultivated the tiny flood⁄plain at the mouth of Khor Bahan and possibly pastured their flocks on the flood plains of two adjacent wadis that did not have populations of their own. This community was the prototype of similar ones that were soon to appear elsewhere in Lower Nubia.

The Khor Bahan graves contained black⁄topped pottery, white

painted and black incised wares, flint knives, stone bowls, lozenge-
shaped slate palettes, disc-shaped maceheads, and ivory ornaments
similar to those of the late Amratian and early Gerzean cultures.
Malachite was used for eye cosmetic and needles and other small objects
were made of copper. The graves and burials were in no way different
from those of Upper Egypt. Bodies were wrapped in 'straw' matting
and halfa grass. Some linen was found but kilts and long fringed garments were usually made of leather. Several baskets filled with unidentified seeds and fruit were also found. Finally, bones of cattle and
goats indicate a subsistence economy similar to that of Upper Egypt.[27]

It has been suggested that the Khor Bahan site marks the beginning of
an expansion of Egyptian settlers into Lower Nubia that was to extend
southward throughout the A-Group period. Such expansion might be
the result of the population increase that can be noted in Egypt during
the Predynastic period. Alternatively Khor Bahan and later sites could
have been colonies that the Gerzean states to the north established to
secure raw materials from sub-Saharan Africa. The original settlers also
may have been Egyptians fleeing the political struggles that preceded
the unification of Egypt.

On the other hand, Junker noted features that distinguish even the
early A-Group culture from the Predynastic cultures of Upper Egypt.
One example is the locally made black-mouthed pottery which is of
rougher fabric and has a narrower black lip than does its Egyptian
black-topped prototype.[28] It has also been observed that A-Group stone
tools are somewhat similar to Abkan ones.[29] This suggests that in spite
of close physical similarities between the prehistoric populations of
Upper Egypt and Lower Nubia, the A-Group culture probably
developed among an indigenous population that was in contact with
Upper Egypt and much influenced from that direction. While the
poverty of Lower Nubia may have been reason enough for the Egyptian
kings to have established the southern frontier of the Pharaonic state at
Aswan, they would have had an additional reason for doing so, if
already at this period the Egyptian language did not extend south of the
Aswan region. We have no means of telling to what linguistic family
the language of the A-Group belonged, although tenuous arguments
have been advanced in favour of both Kushitic and Eastern Sudanic.[30]

While trade goods show that close contacts were maintained between

Fig. 5

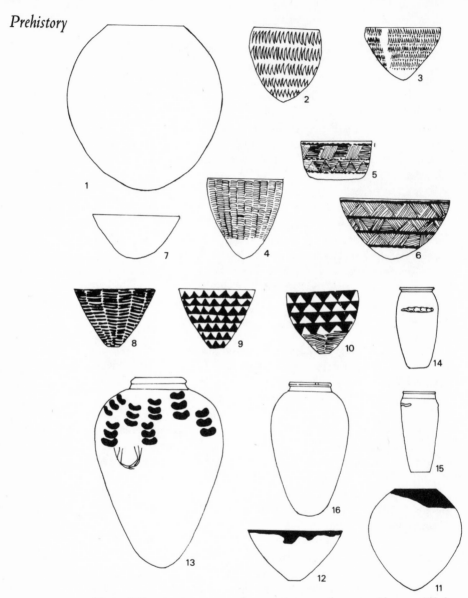

Fig. 5   A-Group pottery: 1, 2, 3, 4 brown coarse or smooth ware; 5, 6 brown-and-black
plain polished ware; 7 red polished plain ware; 8, 9, 10 brown-and-black 'egg shell' ware;
11 black-topped, brown or red rippled ware; 12 black-topped, red-polished plain ware;
Egyptian hard pink unpolished ware (imported to Nubia) 13, 16 wine jars, 14, 15 wavy-
handled jars (after Nordström 1972: pls 36–48)

Nubia and Upper Egypt, Nubia not unexpectedly failed to keep abreast of its richer and more populous neighbour. The separate development of the two regions soon produced a distinctive culture in Lower Nubia in which traits survived that had become obsolete in Upper Egypt. The A-Group has been divided into three stages: Early, Classic, and Terminal. These are distinguished in part on the basis of Egyptian trade goods.[31] The first stage, which is contemporary with the early and middle Gerzean culture in Egypt is represented by sites that extend from Kubanieh in the north to Sayala in the south. The most important area of settlement was the rich plain at Dakka. This region may have been the original Wawat, the name applied to the northern part of Lower Nubia in Egyptian texts of a few centuries later. South of Sayala only a few widely scattered sites of Early A-Group date have been located.

The Classic and Terminal A-Group sites are contemporary with the late Gerzean culture and the beginning of the First Dynasty. Early A-Group localities continued to be inhabited but a large number of sites were now spread throughout Lower Nubia and there were even a few in the northern part of the Batn el-Hagar.[32] The expansion of the A-Group, which produced the most extensive cultural horizon yet seen in Lower Nubia, seems to have involved the assimilation of the Qadan and Khartoum Variant cultures of southern Lower Nubia. As a result of this process, a few pottery traits and other characteristics of these earlier cultures persisted in the A-Group sites of southern Lower Nubia.[33]

Little is known about the subsistence patterns of the A-Group. Remains of wheat, barley, and leguminous plants such as peas and lentils have been found in living sites while date stones, perhaps from wild trees, have been discovered in A-Group graves. Bones of sheep, goats, cattle, and dogs have been identified and cattle dung was used to temper pottery. While some archaeologists have emphasized the importance of cattle breeding during A-Group and C-Group times, it appears that sheep and goats were of greater practical importance to the A-Group than were cattle, although the latter were herded by the inhabitants of the Red Sea Hills. Drawings of elephant, giraffe, gazelle, and antelope on A-Group pottery and the use of ivory and ostrich egg shells to manufacture ornaments suggest that the A-Group people were

35

still in contact with these fauna. In spite of the decline in stone tools, it appears likely that hunting and fowling continued to be of considerable importance.[34] Wild plants and fresh water molluscs were also gathered and fish hooks made of copper were used for the first time. These were probably imported from Egypt and suggest that a new fishing technique had been adopted in addition to the harpoons and fish traps that are attested formerly in Lower Nubia (although there were bone fish hooks at Shaheinab).[35] In general, the diet appears to have consisted of cereals, vegetables, and possible dairy produce, supplemented by fish and meat.

The typical A-Group settlements were small camp sites, some of which contain multiple occupation layers. These sites seem to have been occupied by a small band or extended family. Fireplaces are scattered randomly through the occupation layers but there are few structural remains. Reed mats fastened on to poles probably provided shelter; as they did in Upper Nubia in the last century. Only a few sites show traces of rough dry stone masonry. Rock shelters were also inhabited where available.

In spite of the unsettled, almost nomadic conditions that are suggested by these habitation sites, other evidence indicates greater stability. A-Group cemeteries contain up to one hundred or more graves and secondary burials were placed in a large number of graves some time after the original interment. This seems to indicate that a band or extended family used the same cemetery over a considerable period of time. Possibly each such group owned and exploited a specific territory adjacent to the river bank. While most of the year their camp sites were by the river, during the inundation they retreated to the edge of the floodplain producing the sites that archaeologists have been able to recover. No cemeteries or living sites of special importance are associated with the Early A-Group culture, which suggests a simple political organization centered on the individual small band and its headman.

The A-Group culture shared with the Predynastic Egyptian ones a concern with burial rituals and grave goods that was hitherto foreign to Nubia. Although wind erosion has badly deflated most cemeteries, the discovery of circular stone superstructures covering the graves at Tunqala West suggests what the general covering for graves may have been like.[36] Most graves were dug in the high gravels or silts along the edge of the flood plain, were oval or sub-rectangular in plan, and were covered

Fig. 6

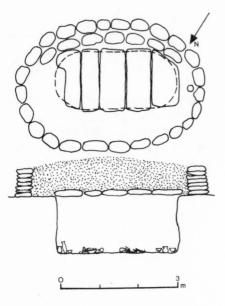

Fig. 6 Plan and section of A-Group grave from Tunqala West, Lower Nubia (after Smith 1962: fig. 14)

with sticks and matting or stone slabs to permit bodies to be placed in the graves at different times. There is no evidence of retainer sacrifice at this time that might otherwise account for these multiple burials. Bodies were wrapped in leather or fur pelts and sometimes were laid on a grass or reed mat. They were normally buried in a contracted position, on the left side and with the head facing south; the same orientation as that of Predynastic Upper Egypt. The bodies appear sometimes to have been sprinkled with red ochre. Numerous storage jars, grinding implements, and pottery dishes were buried with the dead as well as personal orna-ments. Many of these items were of Egyptian manufacture. No im-ported or locally made goods can be regarded solely as funerary goods, however, since the same types of artefacts are found in habitation sites.

Plate 2

A part from the cemeteries there is very little evidence that bears upon the religious beliefs of the A-Group. Some of the female pottery figurines found in graves may have been meant to represent the dead and to assure their eternal vitality,[37] but as a group they are susceptible to varying interpretations, not all of which are of a religious nature. A-Group drawings in the Painted Rock Shelter at Korosko suggest that it may have been a ledge shrine like the one at Gebel Agg that dates from the time of the New Kingdom. While there are traces of occupation at the Painted Shelter, cooking appears to have been done in a separate shallower cave nearby.[38]

A vast range of Egyptian trade goods is found in A-Group cemeteries and camp sites. The ubiquitous Gerzean pottery vessels occur in many shapes and sizes. They probably arrived in Nubia filled with beer, wine, cheese, oil, and perhaps cereals but were valued in their own right because they excelled the local ceramics in strength and hardness. Most if not all of the linen cloth found in A-Group sites was probably of Egyptian origin and a large number of heavy copper tools such as axes, adzes, harpoons, fishhooks, and chisels seem to have been prized as substitutes for locally-manufactured stone and bone tools. Other foreign luxury goods included many stone palettes (others were made locally); stone bowls; beads, pendants, and amulets of faience, stone, and rarely of gold; and metal pigments such as malachite and gelena that were used as face paint. The various species of Mediterranean and Red Sea shells found in Nubian graves may also have come through Egypt, although those from the Red Sea may have been obtained by direct exchange with pastoralists from the Red Sea Hills.

This southward penetration of Egyptian trade goods appears to be correlated with the spectacular development of craft specializations and regional trade that took place in Upper Egypt during the Gerzean period. It is possible that already in Predynastic times Aswan was an important riverine trading centre on the northern limits of Nubia. From there, Egyptian goods may have passed from tribe to tribe south into Nubia.[39] More likely, however, Egyptian ships, some of which

Fig. 7

may be portrayed in rock carvings throughout Nubia, carried Egyptian goods to trading stations at least as far south as the Second Cataract. Nordström has suggested that a complex of over 500 storage vessels, largely of Egyptian provenance, that was excavated at Khor Daud at the north end of the Dakka plain was a bartering place where the Egyptians exchanged goods with nearby A-Group settlements and with the cattle nomads from the Eastern Desert.[40] A rock shelter near Wadi Halfa which contained large amounts of Egyptian pottery may also indicate Egyptian activity near the Second Cataract.[41]

There is no direct evidence concerning what Egyptian traders sought in exchange from the Nubians. A-Group artefacts are almost non-existent in Egyptian sites suggesting that, as in later times, the Egyptians were seeking raw materials. Apart from a few cattle and hippopotamus tusks, Lower Nubia probably produced little that was valued by the Egyptians and certainly not enough to pay for the vast amount of Egyptian goods that were being imported in the late Predynastic period. This suggests that the Nubians were profiting from their position astride the principal trade route along which the highly prized ivory, ebony, incense, vegetable oils, and leopard and panther skins could move north to supply a growing Egyptian market. The prime importance of the ivory trade at this time may explain Aswan's original name, Abu or Elephant Town.[42] So long as there was no strongly centralized authority either in Upper Egypt or in Dongola to finance and control direct long distance trade, the Nubians living south of Aswan could either trade raw materials northward in return for Egyptian produce or charge Egyptian traders transit duties for safe passage along the Nile. The profits derived from these activities may have laid the foundation for the evident prosperity of the A-Group. It is possible that by importing food, the A-Group were able to expand in numbers beyond the carrying capacity of their own subsistence economy. Yet this would have left the A-Group extremely vulnerable to any disruption of trade.

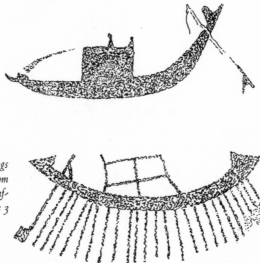

Fig. 7 Boat engravings of Predynastic type from Sabu, Upper Nubia (after Chittick 1962: figs 3 and 1)

39

CHAPTER III
The A-Group and the Old Kingdom

THE EMERGENCE OF THE PHARAONIC STATE

Some Egyptologists maintain that Egypt was politically united 150 years before the start of the First Dynasty, c. 3100 BC.[1] There is, however, no evidence of a major transformation of the country at that time. A trend towards unification among the various Gerzean states was no doubt a feature of the late Gerzean period, but the far-reaching social, economic, and cultural changes that took place around the beginning of the First Dynasty support the traditional view that Egypt's political unification took place just prior to that time. However they gained control over the whole of the Nile Valley north of Aswan, the Pharaohs of the First Dynasty delighted to portray themselves as conquerors, triumphing over supine or dead enemies and carrying off booty, often in the form of livestock.

The rapid development of arts and crafts under the patronage of this newly powerful royal court stimulated a demand for exotic raw materials on an unprecedented and rapidly accelerating scale. Even if control over foreign trade was not specifically claimed as a royal prerogative at this time, the demands of the court so far outstripped those of any other Egyptian consumers that for all practical purposes this trade can be regarded as a royal monopoly. From the beginning of the First Dynasty there is evidence of an elaborate system of accounting and taxation that

Fig. 8 Wooden label of King Aha (First Dynasty) (after Emery 1961 : fig. 11)

Fig. 9 Egyptian relief from Gebel Shaikh Suleiman (after Arkell 1950)

must have placed much of the surplus wealth of Egypt at the disposal of the king and made him the primary source of largess within Egypt. Royally sponsored land reclamation projects, combined with improved internal order and a storage system to provide against local or seasonal crop failure may explain why, in spite of increasing inequalities in the distribution of wealth, even the poor appear to have been more prosperous during the Early Dynastic Period (3100–2700 BC) than they had been previously.[2]

The long-term effects of the unification of Egypt upon Lower Nubia were quite different. An ivory label of King Aha on which a prisoner is apparently identified by the bow sign (*Stj*) traditionally used for Nubia has been interpreted as evidence of military action in the south at the beginning of the First Dynasty. It is possible, however, that in this instance Stj-land refers to the region between Gebel es-Silsila and the First Cataract and that the label alludes to action designed to secure the southern frontier of Egypt at Aswan.[3] A fortress marking this frontier appears to have existed on Elephantine Island at Aswan as early as the reign of King Huni (*c.* 2600 BC).[4] Of much greater importance is a fine royal relief that was carved on Gebel Shaikh Suleiman, on the west bank of the Nile near the foot of the Second Cataract. The relief depicts a Nubian prisoner bound to the prow of an Egyptian ship. To the right a second bound figure is designated by a *Stj*-bow. Corpses lie in the water beneath the ship while a bird sign and another unidentified glyph surmounting the sign for a village or region seem to identify where the action was taking place. Although Helck has recently challenged the attribution of this scene to the reign of King Djer, it certainly dates about the beginning of the First Dynasty.[5]

Fig. 8

Plate 3

Fig. 9

The A-Group and the Old Kingdom

THE CLIMAX AND EXTINCTION OF THE A-GROUP

Plate 4

Despite these suggestions of Egyptian military activity in Lower Nubia, the Terminal A-Group period, which was contemporary with the end of the Gerzean period and the early part of the First Dynasty, appears to have been one of marked prosperity. It saw the culmination of trends already evident in the Classic A-Group period. Everywhere, except in the vicinity of the First Cataract, there appears to have been an increase in the number of settlements, especially in the far south. Near Afyeh a settlement of this period contained several rectangular houses built of dry stone masonry. The largest had six rooms with door openings at the corners and mud floors reinforced with pebbles. Another consisted of two rooms with outside doors facing north. The site stretched for at least 150 metres across a desert bluff between two wadis.[6] The lack of similar houses elsewhere suggests that this site might have been one of unusual importance, perhaps the residence of a local chieftain.

The possibility that the growing prosperity of Lower Nubia had enhanced the power of local leaders is reinforced by finds made in Cemetery 137, south of Sayala. Firth believed this cemetery to be the burial ground of an important local leader and his family and Helene Kantor has dated the richest grave to the early part of the First Dynasty.[7] The graves were large and of a form common to all the more prosperous interments in Nubia at this time. They consisted of sub-rectangular pits dug into the alluvium and roofed over with sandstone slabs of consider-able dimensions. As usual, each grave contained several burials. The funerary offerings of the richest grave included several stone vessels, a number of heavy copper axes, bar ingots and chisels of copper, a dipper made of banded slate, two immense double-bird-shaped palettes, a lion's head of rose quartz covered with green glaze, a mica mirror, and two maces with gold plated handles. A series of animals portrayed in low relief on the handle of the small mace was executed in the same style as animals found on slate palettes from the reign of Narmer, making it one of the masterpieces of Early Dynastic art. Unfortunately, the mace was stolen from the Egyptian Museum soon after it was discovered and it has not been recovered.[8]

It is likely that as the Nile trade became more important, a limited number of locations along the river emerged as major centres of exchange, where bands from neighbouring localities could assemble to barter for

Fig. 10

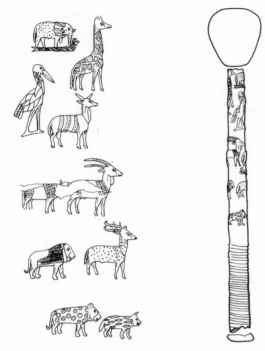

Fig. 10 Gold-handled Egyptian mace from A-Group grave near Sayala, Lower Nubia (after Firth 1927)

Egyptian goods. Whether long distance trade was with Egyptians or with other Nubians, overcoming the difficulties involved in dealing with strangers required elaborate diplomacy and exchanges of presents. All parties would have found it advantageous for the experienced leaders of the bands living closest to the trading centres to regulate the trade that went on at them. These leaders were perhaps also able to monopolize the tolls on goods that passed through their territory. By distributing most of the goodwill presents they received among their followers, such leaders would have greatly enhanced their prestige with these people. Eventually, such activities may have transformed autonomous bands into broader economically linked tribal groupings. The leaders of such groupings and their families were able to display their superior status by living in more elaborately constructed houses and having more lavish grave goods than did other members of the A-Group.[9]

There is also evidence of greater cultural complexity in Lower Nubia

43

in the Terminal A-Group period. Among the characteristic artefacts are handsome conical bowls of a thin 'egg-shell' fabric, black on the inside and slipped on the outside with pink or cream and painted with dark red lines in patterns that often resemble basketry. This pottery is the work of skilled specialists, whose existence is not otherwise attested by A-Group artefacts. A few Egyptian-style cylinder seals that appear to be of A-Group manufacture were probably used to mark possessions. These hint at a growing concern with private property.[10]

Plate 5

That A-Group prosperity reached its peak at the beginning of the First Dynasty suggests that early raids, such as the one commemorated at Gebel Shaikh Suleiman, may not have been directed against the whole of Lower Nubia. They may have been undertaken by the Egyptian king to support Nubian allies and trading partners against their enemies. It is also likely that at least some of the Egyptian goods that entered Lower Nubia in the late Gerzean period and at the start of the First Dynasty were payments made to Nubian mercenaries who, as in later times, served in the Egyptian army. It is tempting to think of the maces in Cemetery 137 as gifts to a Nubian leader for the role that he and his men had played in the wars that had united Egypt.

Hardly any Egyptian goods manufactured later than the early First Dynasty have been found in A-Group sites in Lower Nubia; nor have any native sites been located that are demonstrably contemporary with the rest of the Early Dynastic period or the early Old Kingdom. Reisner interpreted his B-Group as an attenuated and impoverished survival of the A-Group that was contemporary with the Old Kingdom, but Harry Smith has since demonstrated that the graves originally assigned to this culture were misdated; for the most part being badly plundered or very poor A-Group ones.[11] Only the small amount of Nubian pottery found in the Old Kingdom Egyptian settlement at Buhen (some of it associated with squatter-like huts) may indicate a limited survival of the A-Group during the Old Kingdom. Even that pottery may have been carried to the site by Nubian prisoners or traders whose homes were in Upper Nubia. For all practical purposes, the A-Group appears to have vanished from Lower Nubia before the end of the First Dynasty.

There is evidence of a diminution in the volume of the Nile flood during the First Dynasty which may be correlated with a lowering of the floodplain in Lower Nubia from the maximum of 6 to 7 metres above the present level, which was reached between *c.* 4000 and 3000 BC (the Qadrus Aggradation).[12] While these events may have adversely affected Lower Nubia more than they did Egypt, it is impossible to attribute the total disappearance of the A-Group in Lower Nubia entirely to natural causes. Nor is there explicit evidence of Egyptian military activity in Lower Nubia after the early First Dynasty.

It has recently been suggested that as the Egyptian economy became more centralized during the First Dynasty, the multicentric trade that had been carried on with Lower Nubia in earlier times was broken off, destroying the economic base on which the A-Group culture depended.[13] It is likely that Egypt for the first time possessed the economic organization to carry on direct trade with the south, thereby circumventing Lower Nubian middlemen and toll masters. An increasing demand for raw materials from the south also may have made direct contact with that area more urgent than it had been formerly. Evidence from within Egypt suggests that royal power increased during the early reigns of the

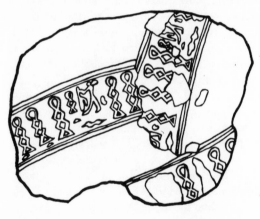

Fig. 11 Jar sealing from Toshka West, Lower Nubia, with seal reconstructed (after Simpson 1963: fig. 39)

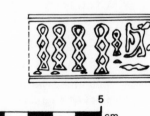

0   5
▬▬▬▬▬▬▬▬▬▬ cm.

45

Fig. 11

First Dynasty, at the expense of former local rulers.[14] The Early Dynastic jar-sealings found in A-Group sites make it just possible that high ranking officials may have engaged in private trade in Lower Nubia at the start of the First Dynasty. The establishment of centralized control over such trade may have put an end to such activities.[15]

While this would seriously have undermined the prosperity of the A-Group, it is difficult to account for the disappearance of all sedentary life in Lower Nubia in terms of this economic breakdown. In spite of the lack of evidence, we must therefore accept the possibility that Egyptian military intervention to protect trade routes to the south was in part responsible for the final disappearance of the A-Group. Some Nubians may have been deported to Egypt, some may have become pastoralists in the region between Lower Nubia and the Red Sea Hills, and some may have retreated farther south.

NUBIA UNDER THE OLD KINGDOM

A fragmentary victory stela of King Khasekhem from Hierakonpolis hints at Egyptian military activities in Nubia towards the end of the Early Dynastic period.[16] It has been suggested that the large bricks that were used to construct the lowest levels of the Egyptian townsite at Buhen indicate that there may have been an Egyptian colony at the foot of the Second Cataract as early as the Second Dynasty, although the town may in fact date from the Third Dynasty. It has also been suggested that several ovens found at Buhen were used to smelt copper, but it does not follow from this that Buhen was established to exploit an as yet undiscovered local source of copper, although Egyptian prospectors appear to have made their way as far south as Kulb, in the Batn el-Hagar, sometime during the Old Kingdom.[17] More likely Buhen was founded as a base for carrying on trade with the south. From there it was possible for the largest ships to sail north to the First Cataract; while, because of cataracts and the Batn el-Hagar, large-scale trade with the south de-pended upon overland transportation. Although it is not certain that Buhen was occupied continuously in the interval, by the Fourth Dynasty (c. 2620–2480 BC) the original town had been replaced by a new one apparently fortified with rough stone walls and a dry moat. Numerous despatch seals found within the town indicate that com-munication with Egypt was maintained on a regular basis. These seals

Plate 7

bear the names of Kings Khafre and Menkaure of the Fourth Dynasty and Userkaf, Sahure, Neferirkare, and Niuserre of the Fifth Dynasty (*c.* 2480–2340 B C).[18]

The Palermo Stone, a year-by-year record of all the kings from the First through the Fifth Dynasties, reports that Sneferu, the first king of the Fourth Dynasty, carried out a raid in Nubia that resulted in the capture of 7000 people and 200,000 domesticated animals. It has been argued that the high proportion of beasts to humans indicates that he was attacking pastoralists.[19] The archaeological evidence makes it highly unlikely that this booty or anything like it could have come from Lower Nubia; nor, unless the figures are greatly exaggerated, does it seem plausible that this military expedition was undertaken to prevent the infiltration of small groups northward. Instead, it seems likely to have been directed against tribesmen living to the south of Buhen and had as its objective to secure trade routes as far south as the Dongola Reach.[20] Buhen may have been the launching point for this expedition.

Plate 6

Nubians who are attested as titled servants of Fifth Dynasty officials may have been the descendants of captives taken by Sneferu, although Nubians continued to enter Egypt throughout the Old Kingdom as prisoners, slaves, or bowmen recruits for the Egyptian army and police force. In the decree of King Pepi I protecting the dependents of Sneferu's two pyramids, several clauses specifically forbid interference by these 'peaceful Nubians'.[21]

Little is known about other Egyptian activities in Lower Nubia during the Fourth and Fifth Dynasties, which marked the high point of the Old Kingdom. Although Säve-Söderbergh has argued that traces of Old Kingdom settlement that Firth and Steindorff believed existed at Ikkur and Aniba were not conclusive, O'Connor accepts the Old Kingdom pottery found at Quban as evidence that an Old Kingdom settlement existed in that area.[22] It would have been useful and probably was necessary to have a number of Egyptian settlements between Aswan and Buhen, where boats could dock for provisions or seek protection from harassment by wandering pastoralists. During the Fourth and Fifth Dynasties, diorite was surface-quarried about 80 kilometres to the northwest of Toshka in a desolate, cairnmarked patch of desert euphemistically called the 'Snaring Place of King Khufu'. The stone for the famous statues found in Khafre's mortuary temple at Giza came

Plate 8

from there. When Engelbach investigated these quarries in 1933, he found there the names of Khufu, Redjedef, Sahure, and Djedkare-Isesi – all kings of the Fourth and Fifth Dynasties – as well as the names of rulers of the Middle Kingdom.[23] Semi-precious stone was also quarried at the same location. It is likely that the ancient track leading to the quarries left the Nile at Toshka West. At the latter spot a fragmentary Old Kingdom stela and a Middle Kingdom one that refers specifically to quarrying operations have been found.[24] No evidence of defensive works occurs either at Toshka or at the quarries, which suggests that there was no serious opposition to Egyptian activities either along the river or in the adjacent Western Desert at this time. Egyptian surveillance may have been largely responsible for the failure of sedentary settlement to revive in Lower Nubia during the Fourth and Fifth Dynasties.

There is no evidence, either archaeological or historical, that the Egyptian settlement at Buhen was inhabited after the reign of Djedkare-Isesi, the last king but one of the Fifth Dynasty. No royal names from later in the Old Kingdom are recorded in the Toshka quarries while the use of alabaster, which is found locally in Middle Egypt, largely replaced that of diorite. This suggests that by the beginning of the Sixth Dynasty (*c.* 2340 B C) Nubia was free from Egyptian occupation. The relaxation of Egyptian control seems to have come about as a result of the growing independence of Upper Egypt, which was apparent by the reign of Teti I, the first king of the Sixth Dynasty. Prior to that time a shift of power to a provincially based nobility is indicated by a decline in the size of royal tombs and a tendency for the tombs of the nobility to be located independently of those of the reigning monarch. The decline of Egyptian control in Nubia seems related to a general decline in royal power.

Plate 9

The Early C-Group

During the Sixth Dynasty an indigenous settled population began to reappear in Lower Nubia. It was associated with the C-Group culture that was to persist in Lower Nubia into the New Kingdom. Although the C-Group is known primarily from cemeteries, recent studies have helped to clarify the chronology and internal development of this culture. Only the first stage of C-Group development (Bietak's phases Ia and Ib), which lasted into the first half of the Twelfth Dynasty, will be considered in this chapter.[1]

In general, C-Group cemeteries are somewhat larger than those of the A-Group, although the population appears to have been quite small in early C-Group times. Bodies were usually buried in round or oval graves. They were laid on the right side, in a semi-flexed position, the head pointing east. Graves were covered with stone rings filled with

Plate 10

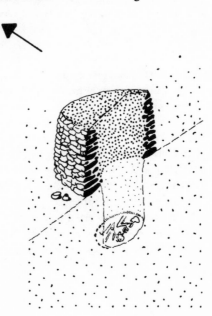

Fig. 12 Early C-Group grave (after Steindorff 1937)

49

The Early C-Group

Fig. 13 Early C-Group pottery: 1–6 black incised ware with white encrustation; 7 black-topped ware; 8, 9 red-slipped jars (after Bietak 1968: pls 2, 3)

Fig. 12

Fig. 13

Plate 11

gravel, similar to those used by the A-Group. At the beginning of the early C-Group these superstructures were small and built of well fitted stones but later they were larger and the stones not so well fitted as previously. Later many grave pits were roughly rectangular. Offerings were left in pottery bowls against the east side of the stone superstructures. The pottery consisted of black-mouthed bowls similar to those of the A-Group and black vessels covered on the outside with incised decorations accented with white paint. The earliest bowls tended to be shallow; later ones were hemispherical. Occasionally, rough sandstone slabs or stelae engraved with representations of cows were erected in the cemeteries. A marked break with earlier traditions is the absence of stone palettes or other evidence of a concern with eye paint, which featured prominently in the A-Group culture and in Egypt.

At least two small habitation sites are associated with the early

C-Group. One was on the south side of Khor Abu Bakr at Sayala West. The largest structure at this site was an oval compound 25 metres in diameter. There were at least four circular huts inside the compound, none more than 6 metres across, while five more circular huts were located outside it. Bietak argues that the stones outlining the perimeters of the compound and huts supported walls of thorns or reeds, the stony surface of the plateau making it impossible to drive stakes into the ground. The pottery from this settlement resembles what is believed to be the earliest C-Group pottery from cemetery N at Aniba. Egyptian sealings from Khor Abu Bakr are apparently of the First Intermediate Period.[2] In the lowest level of the stratified village site excavated by the Ernst von Sieglin Expedition at Aniba three tent circles were dis-covered, each 4 to 5 metres in diameter. These had a centre pole, a fire-place off centre, and a ring of smaller posts marking the perimeter. Traces were found of the skins that had covered these tents, whose entrances did not face in any one direction.[3]

Fig. 14

Although the remains of these structures are more substantial than those found in all but the most important A-Group settlements, they

Fig. 14 Early C-Group residential compound at Sayala West (after Bietak 1966: pl. 12)

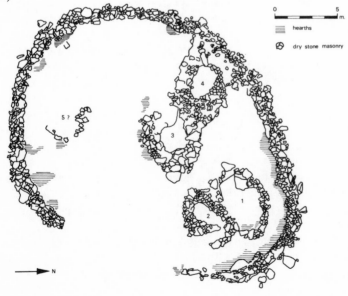

0   5
      m.

≡ hearths

⊗ dry stone masonry

N

suggest that during early C-Group times the population of Lower Nubia continued to move about from season to season. The hut circles each seem to have housed a single family with a number of related ones forming a lineage based settlement. Recent African parallels suggest that the compound at Khor Abu Bakr may have been inhabited by a man, his several wives and their children. One of the huts inside the compound was a storehouse; probably used communally by its inhabitants or by the whole settlement.

Although food remains from C-Group sites have been little studied, the emphasis on cattle on early C-Group stelae and as motifs for pottery decoration and rock carvings has led many archaeologists to assert that the C-Group were cattle pastoralists. Only a small number of cattle could ever have been pastured in Lower Nubia, however, and most of the animal bones from the Khor Abu Bakr site were those of sheep. The few cattle that were kept seem to have been status symbols and a focus of sentiment rather than the basis of the local economy.[4] In agriculture, the same crops were probably grown in much the same way as they had been by the A-Group.

C-GROUP ORIGINS

The origins of the C-Group have been the subject of much debate. Only fragmentary information is available about the cultural sequences in the deserts on either side of Lower Nubia; however, similarities have been noted between C-Group pottery and sherds found in the Wadi Howar and elsewhere in the Western Desert. Graffiti from the Western Desert featuring cattle with vertical lines across their bodies are also allegedly similar to rock carvings found in Lower Nubia and representations of cattle on C-Group pottery. Further C-Group affinities have been noted east of the Nile; in the hills around Port Sudan and farther south at Agordat in the Tokar Delta. On the basis of these findings, it has been proposed that the C-Group culture was brought into Lower Nubia either by Beja from the Eastern Desert or by Libyan invaders from the west. It is argued that increasing desiccation of adjacent grazing lands forced these people into the Nile Valley towards the end of the Old Kingdom.[5]

Recent work in Upper Nubia indicates continuity between the A-Group (or a local equivalent) and whatever variant of the C-Group existed in that area. It also appears likely that the Kerma culture of Upper Nubia, which was closely related to the C-Group, developed from this local C-Group variant.[6] This suggests that during the third and second millennia BC a common pottery tradition (the C-Horizon) was shared by various groups inhabiting the Nile Valley and adjacent regions. The black-topped pottery that bulks so large in the C-Horizon almost certainly had its origin in Predynastic Upper Egypt. Black incised pottery was also known in Predynastic Upper Egypt, although its relationship to the black incised ware of the C-Horizon is uncertain because of the unimportance of this pottery in the intervening A-Group; however, black ware incised with patterns closely resembling those of C-Horizon pottery has been found in the Omdurman culture of the Khartoum region. This culture has many parallels with the A-Group and is believed to be of about the same age.[7] Until more is known about the C-Horizon, it is dangerous to relate its individual cultures by postulating hypothetical migrations. Specific differences can be noted among the C-Group pottery of Lower Nubia, the Kerma pottery of Upper Nubia, and the pottery of the Pan-Grave culture, believed to be associated with the Medjay nomads of the Eastern Desert. The Agordat culture of the Ethiopian border seems to be yet another distinctive manifestation of this horizon.[8] It is therefore possible that, as with the Khartoum Mesolithic and Khartoum Neolithic Horizons, similar pottery types were adopted by different peoples over a wide area. If some of these groups were semi-nomadic pastoralists, conditions would have been optimal for the spread and maintenance of this horizon.

It is not impossible that as the Egyptians grew less vigilant, pastoralists from the Eastern or Western Desert began to settle in Lower Nubia. Whether these were the same people who had lived in Lower Nubia in A-Group times or a completely new ethnic group cannot now be ascertained. The argument that the C-Group must have originated somewhere to the west of Lower Nubia because all of the earliest C-Group sites occur on the west bank of the Nile is statistically invalid; the sample is very small and sites of all periods occur more frequently along the richer west bank.[9] Alternatively, it is possible that the C-Group culture evolved from the 'A-Group' of Upper Nubia and that settlers took advantage of relaxed Egyptian control to occupy the more fertile parts of Lower Nubia. Finally, many or all of the C-Group people may be descendants of the A-Group inhabitants of Lower Nubia who remained there as pastoralists during the Old Kingdom and who were able to increase in numbers and re-acquire the trappings of a semi-sedentary culture during the Sixth Dynasty. At present it is impossible to accept as certain any proposed ethnic identification for the C-Group of Lower Nubia. It appears from rock inscriptions that the Egyptians of this period called the northern part of Lower Nubia Wawat; the Tomas area Irtje; and a third district, between there and the Second Cataract, Satju. These toponyms may, however, have been old ones that lacked any ethnographic meaning after the disappearance of the A-Group.

Fig. 15

RELATIONS WITH EGYPT

Although Egyptian goods appear to have been scarce in Nubia throughout most of the Sixth Dynasty (2340–2190 BC), they reached Nubia in considerable quantities at the end of the Old Kingdom and during the First Intermediate Period. Most of the Egyptian pottery found in C-Group sites are round-based, necked vessels that served as containers for liquids and foodstuffs. This suggests that the C-Group were obtaining food from Egypt as the A-Group had done. Numerous seal-amulets occur in C-Group sites and occasionally a skeleton is found holding an Egyptian copper mirror before its face.[10]

The Egyptian abandonment of their settlements in Lower Nubia by the beginning of the Sixth Dynasty, did not mean that they had ceased to be interested in the lands to the south. Manufacturing luxury goods for the Egyptian upper classes required a steady supply of raw materials from sub-Saharan Africa. Egyptian river traffic appears to have continued in Lower Nubia during the first part of the Sixth Dynasty and the names of many Egyptian officials of this period are inscribed on the rocks at Tomas. Three of these officials, Sabi, Tetiankh, and Iri, bore the title 'Overseer of Foreigners' and it has been suggested that one of the duties of Egyptian officials visiting Nubia may have been to recruit Nubians for the Egyptian army.[11] A Sixth Dynasty official named Weni boasted of leading a large army against the Asiatics and 'Sand-Dwellers' who lived to the east of Egypt. Part of this army was made up of Nubians from Wawat, Irtje, and the still more southerly districts of Kaau and Iam, as well as of Medjay recruits from the Eastern Desert.[12]

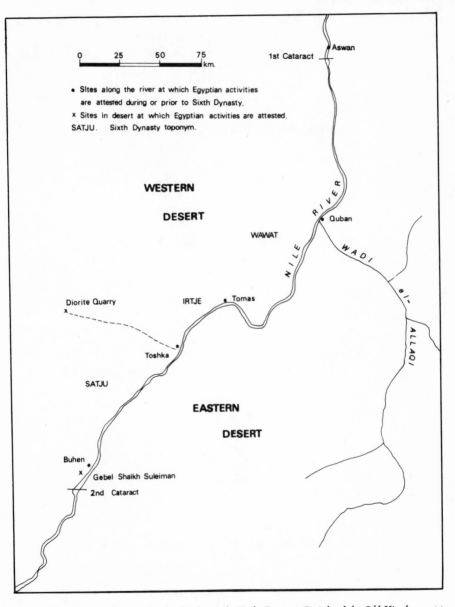

Fig. 15 Egyptian activities in Lower Nubia during the Early Dynastic Period and the Old Kingdom   55

Many of the Egyptian goods appearing in C-Group sites of this period probably were wages paid to Nubian mercenaries or their families.

Early in the reign of Merenre, the third king of the Sixth Dynasty, Weni was made Governor of Upper Egypt; a post originally established to counteract the growing power of the provincial nobles and to ensure the collection of taxes in southern Egypt.[13] In this capacity, Weni led an expedition to the quarries at Aswan to fetch a granite sarcophagus and other building elements for the king's pyramid. Later he cut five navigable channels through the First Cataract and supervised the construction of seven vessels using acacia wood purchased from the chiefs of Wawat, Irtje, Iam, and the Medjay. These boats were presumably used to transport stone from the Aswan quarries. Two inscriptions from the First Cataract record that about this time Merenre visited the frontier and met the chiefs of Wawat, Irtje, and the Medjay. The meeting was conventionally interpreted by the Egyptians as an act of homage by the Nubians, but it was probably a piece of Egyptian diplomacy intended to promote goodwill amongst the tribes living along Egypt's southern border.[14]

THE LAND OF IAM

The principal concern of the Egyptians was to continue their trade with Dongola. In the course of the Sixth Dynasty, control of this trade fell into the hands of the Governors of Aswan who assumed special powers as the 'Keeper of the Door to the South'. These princes supervised expeditions not only up the Nile Valley but also along the Red Sea to the land of Punt (Ethiopia or Somalia).[15] On his tomb, opposite Aswan, Harkhuf records that, beginning in the reign of Merenre, he personally led four expeditions to the land of Iam to recruit troops and barter for goods there. On the first of these journeys he was accompanied by his father Iri. It is likely that Iri was making his last visit to Iam and was familiarizing his son and successor with the route and introducing him to his Nubian trading partners. Harkhuf returned from his third journey with 300 donkeys laden with incense, ebony, oil, leopard skins, elephant tusks, throwing sticks, and other products. He was guarded by a strong contingent of Iamite recruits who were returning with him for service in the Egyptian army. On his fourth expedition, Harkhuf brought back from Iam a dancing dwarf (hardly a true pigmy) whose

Plate 12

impending arrival delighted the boy king Pepi II. Harkhuf had inscribed on his tomb the text of a royal letter instructing him to make certain that the dwarf reached the king safely.[16]

There has been much speculation about the location of Iam. Harkhuf's journeys each began and ended at the royal court in Memphis and lasted seven to eight months. Sometimes he left the river at Aswan; sometimes he travelled south from Abydos through the Kharga Oasis. Always, however, his goods were carried overland by donkeys. South of Tomas, Harkhuf appears to have approximately followed the course of the river and his journeys carried him far south of the Second Cataract. He and his father thus appear to have been outfitting caravans in Egypt for the same purpose that such caravans had formerly been outfitted at Buhen. The overland journey to Iam was several hundred miles longer but did not involve extra overhead to maintain an outpost at the Second Cataract.[17]

On the basis of the time that Harkhuf says it took him to get to Iam, Edel has calculated that Iam was located in the Kerma Basin above the Third Cataract.[18] This suggestion has won widespread approval and linguistic research has strengthened Edel's claim. Iam may have survived as a toponym or ethnic name (*Irm*) into the Meroitic period. It is also possible that the name endures as part of the modern Kerma.[19] The continuity of this place-name may be a reflection of long-term ethnic continuity in this region. Since Nubian words are recorded for the Dongola area as early as the New Kingdom, speakers of a Nubian language (although possibly not the direct ancestor of modern Nile Nubian) may already have been living in that area as early as the Old Kingdom.[20] As yet there is no archaeological evidence concerning what Harkhuf encountered at the end of his journey. Reisner excavated Sixth Dynasty stone vessels at Kerma and believed that there had been an Egyptian trading post there as early as the Sixth Dynasty. These jars have been interpreted as old ones that the Egyptians traded to the Nubians in the Middle Kingdom or later,[21] although they may be evidence of Old Kingdom contact.

The Harkhuf inscriptions suggest that by the Sixth Dynasty Iam was a prosperous chiefdom whose ruler dealt with Egyptian officials on equal terms. The Kerma Basin could have supported a considerable population and was a convenient collection point for trade goods entering the Dongola Reach from the south. If trade were not carried out under the patronage of a responsible and powerful official, trifling disputes between traders from different ethnic backgrounds might easily have provoked economically disastrous blood feuds. To assure the proper conduct of trade, the Upper Nubians probably agreed that it was best controlled by the ruler of Iam. Egyptians were not allowed to trade within Iam without first obtaining the permission of this ruler. Harkhuf records that when he arrived there for the third time, the ruler was leading a war party against the Libyans of the Western Desert. Harkhuf there-fore went in search of this ruler and 'pacified (*sḥtp*-ed) him so that he praised all the gods for the King of Egypt'. The verb *sḥtp* is ambiguous and some Egyptologists have interpreted it to mean that Harkhuf militarily defeated the ruler of Iam in order to prevent him from doing something that seemed to threaten Egypt's interest.[22] It is difficult, however, to imagine that Harkhuf and his small force would have attacked the leader of a populous group with whom his aim was to conduct business. Instead, it appears that Harkhuf was conforming to established custom by offering presents to the local ruler to gain his permission for a new round of trading and recruiting mercenaries. It is unknown whether this freed Harkhuf to transact business with in-dividual Iamite merchants or all trading had to be carried on with the local ruler. These expeditions provided the Egyptian court with highly desirable produce; therefore Egyptian officials had reason to boast about the diplomatic finesse with which they acted in the service of their king.

The textual evidence strongly contradicts the traditional view that Iam was a little developed, tribal society. Instead it had a ruler who was able to regulate all external trade. The profits derived from this right would have enhanced his position at the apex of an economic re-distributive system and increased his political power. While his subjects were recruited as mercenaries for the Egyptian army, the ruler of Iam was not counted among the Nubian 'chiefs' who owed allegiance to the King of Egypt.[23] At the time of Harkhuf's visit, Iam was probably at a level of development analogous to that of the small states that had evolved in Upper Egypt by early Gerzean times. The latter's develop-ment had been encouraged at least in part by trade with southwestern Asia.[24] It can be speculated that the Iamite chiefdom started to evolve once the Egyptians were trading directly with Dongola from their colony at Buhen.

Harkhuf's records also suggest that the power of the C-Group chiefs of Lower Nubia increased in the course of the Sixth Dynasty. On his second journey he stated that there was a single ruler for Satju and Irtje, but by the time of his third journey one man ruled these regions and Wawat as well. This change possibly indicates the development of a loose tribal confederacy encompassing the whole small and scattered population of Lower Nubia. The early C-Group cemeteries show far less variability in size of graves and quality of grave goods than do those of the late A-Group, which suggests that C-Group society remained strongly tribal and egalitarian. During the Sixth Dynasty, it seems to have been the custom of Egyptian officials to offer presents to Nubian chiefs in order to maintain their goodwill and to ensure a safe passage through Nubia for themselves and their wares. When the principal chief, who seems to have lived in the Tomas area, saw the size of the mercenary force that was returning to Egypt with Harkhuf, he provided Harkhuf with oxen and goats and personally conducted him over the Heights of Irtje (probably across the Korosko Hills to Dakka). The clear implication is that if Harkhuf had not been accompanied by so powerful a force, he would have had to pay dearly for such good treatment.[25]

Relations with Lower Nubia appear to have deteriorated late in the Sixth Dynasty. Mekhu, a prince of Aswan in the reign of Pepi II, died or was killed (it is not clear which) in Lower Nubia and his successor Sabni headed south with 100 donkeys laden with honey, oil, clothes, ointment, and other goods. These appear to have been presents for the Nubians, but whether they were intended to ransom his father's body or to reward them for preserving it is uncertain. Another prince, Pepinakht, records a punitive expedition in which he 'hacked up' Wawat and Irtje, slaying prominent people and carrying off many prisoners. On a second expedition, an unknown time later, Pepinakht was able to persuade two chiefs to visit the Egyptian court and to present some cattle as tribute.[26] While the withdrawal of Egyptian settlement from Buhen northward to the First Cataract permitted a resumption of native settlement in Lower Nubia, a continuing need to protect the trade routes to the Kerma Basin led the Egyptians to alternate between

The Early C-Group

bribery and intimidation in dealing with the C-Group. While Egypt's power to act was weakened by growing decentralization, her capacity to hurt the people of Lower Nubia was still great. Occasional interventions such as those described by Pepinakht probably were sufficient to keep the population low and the economy a semi-sedentary one.

THE FIRST INTERMEDIATE PERIOD

Many factors seem to have contributed to the political fragmentation that overtook Egypt after the 90-year reign of Pepi II. It has been suggested that a series of extraordinarily low Niles between 2180 and 2130 B C undermined the economic basis of Egyptian society.[27] A period of anarchy and bloodshed followed the collapse of the central government, after which Upper Egypt was dominated by two rival royal families who ruled from Herakleopolis and Thebes respectively. About 2040 B C, the Theban ruler Mentuhotep-Sankhibtowe reunited Egypt, ushering in a phase of political unity and economic and cultural prosperity known as the Middle Kingdom. The period between the collapse and reunification of the central power in Egypt is known as the First Intermediate Period.

There is no archaeological evidence that Lower Nubia was adversely affected by the low Niles postulated for the beginning of the First Intermediate Period; but, because of the nature of the archaeological record, important clues may have gone unnoticed. With the collapse of the central government, direct trade with Iam ceased and African luxuries no longer reached the former capital at Memphis. While non-royal graves in Egypt indicate generally greater access to wealth in the First Intermediate Period than during the Old Kingdom, imported luxuries such as lapis lazuli, turquoise, and ivory are everywhere absent or very rare.[28] It is unknown what effect the cessation of direct trade had on Iam, but there is no evidence that thereafter the Lower Nubians played a significant role in trading between Dongola and Egypt.

In spite of this, Egyptian goods abound in C-Group graves of the First Intermediate Period. Although Nubian and other foreign mercenaries plundered native Egyptians during the initial period of anarchy, many Nubians as well as Medjay from the Eastern Desert were recruited during the civil wars that followed and some of these men achieved prominent positions in Egyptian society.[29] A model of a troop of

Nubian bowmen found in a tomb at Assiut in central Egypt and a   Plate 13
reference to Wawat Nubians and Medjay as followers of the ruler of
Hermopolis indicate that Nubian contingents fought for the Herakleopolitan coalition, while a large colony at Gebelein, near Luxor, was no   *Fig. 16*
doubt in the service of the rival Theban dynasts.[30] There was also a
C-Group settlement at Kubanieh, just north of Aswan.[31] Thebes
enjoyed a decided advantage when it came to recruiting more Nubians
and it is no accident that most of the Egyptian pottery found in C-Group
sites of the First Intermediate Period is of the sort that occurs only south of
Matmar and was confined to the Theban sphere of influence. Economic
exchange between the Theban and Herakleopolitan spheres of influence
appears to have been extremely limited until Egypt was reunited.[32]

Fig. 16 Nubian mercenary of the First Inter-
mediate Period as depicted in the tomb of the
Egyptian official Ankhtifi at Moalla, across the
river from Gebelein in Upper Egypt (after
Fischer 1961: fig. 6)

Responsibilities towards mercenaries may explain why Ankhtifi, the ruler of Edfu and Hierakonpolis at the beginning of the First Inter, mediate Period, boasted of having supplied food to the Wawat Nubians during a famine.[33] This may be a literary reference to major famines in Nubia at the start of the First Intermediate Period.

There is evidence of Egyptian military activity later in the First Intermediate Period, which may have had as its objectives to secure the southern border of Egypt and to renew trading links with Dongola. In an inscription from Gebelein, an officer named Djemi boasts of having made Wawat Nubians tributary to the Theban ruler.[34] Royal graffiti found as far south as Abu Simbel appear to record raids into Lower Nubia. The inscription of King Wadjkare at Khor Dehmit has been tentatively attributed to a king of the ephemeral Eighth Dynasty, while the more numerous and sometimes associated graffiti of Kakare, Intef and Iyibkhentre are interpreted as variants of the names of Eleventh Dynasty Theban rulers.[35] Like the raids of the Sixth Dynasty, these campaigns must have served to disrupt the economy of Lower Nubia and keep its population low. It is perhaps incongruous that Nubian mercenaries served rulers who were attacking their homeland, but the loyalties of these soldiers were probably narrow and they did not mind attacking districts other than their own. The prospect of employment and booty must have attracted many Nubians north into Egypt, while Egyptian raids made life difficult for those who remained behind.

Plate 14

Mentuhotep's programme to restore the prestige of the Egyptian central government involved repressing various tribal peoples who had taken advantage of Egypt's weakened condition to raid its borders. He sought to secure trade routes and to make the oases and outlying quarries safe for Egyptian work parties. Expeditions were sent against the inhabitants of the Sinai Peninsula (and perhaps points farther east), the Libyans of the Western Desert, and the pastoralists of the Eastern Desert.[36]

A decline in the amount of Egyptian goods reaching Lower Nubia seems to date from this period.[37] The reimposition of state controls over trade and a diminished demand for mercenaries no doubt explain this development, which in many respects repeated what happened at the beginning of the Early Dynastic Period. A fragmentary inscription from near El Ballas, north of Thebes, refers to a military campaign in which Mentuhotep annexed Wawat and received the submission of desert tribesmen.[38] A series of graffiti recorded by a Nubian mercenary named Tjehemau a short distance above Aswan states that the king sailed in person as far south as Ben, which, perhaps wrongly, has been interpreted as a reference to Buhen.[39] Mentuhotep's chancellor travelled to Lower Nubia several times and one of his inscriptions refers to ships assigned for service in Nubia.[40]

While the natives of Lower Nubia were no doubt compelled to pay tribute, at least on an intermittent basis, the precise nature of Egyptian influence in Lower Nubia towards the end of the Eleventh Dynasty is unclear. There is no evidence of military occupation; even the graffiti bearing Eleventh Dynasty names that occur with considerable frequency around Buhen are now believed to date from the early Twelfth Dynasty.[41] Mentuhotep was presumably interested in securing the safety of the granite quarries and amethyst mines near Aswan. He may also have sought to exploit natural resources farther south and a possible expedition to the Kurkur Oasis suggests an interest in controlling the trade routes to Iam.[42] On the whole, however, Egyptian policy in Lower Nubia during the Eleventh Dynasty appears to resemble what had been followed in the Sixth Dynasty and during the First Intermediate Period.

Plate 15

CHAPTER V

The Middle Kingdom

THE EGYPTIAN OCCUPATION OF LOWER NUBIA

A few years after the death of Mentuhotep his line came to an end and the throne was mounted by Amenemhet I, founder of the Twelfth Dynasty. He may be the same Amenemhet who was vizier under the last king of the Eleventh Dynasty. The semi-fictional Prophecy of Neferti implies that his mother was a woman of To-Stj; which probably meant that she was from the Aswan district rather than a Nubian.[1] In becoming Pharaoh, Amenemhet appears to have worked out a *modus vivendi* that left considerable power in the hands of the hereditary nobility. Nevertheless, emulating the Pharaohs of the Old Kingdom, he shifted the capital from Thebes to Itj-towe ('Possessor of the Two Lands') near Memphis and consciously began to revive the court culture of that former era.[2] His Horus name *Wehammeswe* ('Repeater of Births') indicates that he thought of himself as inaugurating a major new era. Although Amenemhet was murdered in his palace after a 30-year reign, his heirs were to rule Egypt for over 200 years.

Much of Amenemhet's reign seems to have been preoccupied with settling the internal affairs of Egypt. Yet, an inscription at Korosko records that in the penultimate year of his reign (which coincided with the ninth regnal year of his son and co-regent Senwosret I) he arrived 'to overthrow Wawat'. He is said to have waged war against the Medjay of the Eastern Desert and the Toshka diorite quarries may have been worked again by the end of his reign.[3]

Apparently after his father's death, Senwosret I erected a series of forts in Lower Nubia and garrisoned them with Egyptian soldiers.[4] This was the first settlement of Nubia by Egyptians since the end of the Fifth Dynasty and marked the beginning of a new phase in relations between Egypt and its southern hinterland. While little is known about the building sequences of the Middle Kingdom forts in Nubia, the first round bastioned, mud brick forts at Ikkur, Quban, and Aniba were probably erected in the reign of Senwosret I.[5] There is textual evidence that a new fortress at Buhen was garrisoned at this time and Smith has suggested that the central town at Kor, just south of Buhen, was also occupied. This settlement seems to have been a caravanserai for overland travel to the south and a residence for sailors, porters, and craftsmen attached to the Buhen colony.[6] Forts may already have been established as far south as Semna. Nubia was placed under the control of the prince of Aswan, Serenput. In his tomb he described himself as 'Great Controller of Nubia' and 'Overseer of all Foreign Lands'.[7]

A magnificent sandstone stela erected at Buhen by General Mentuhotep appears to record an expedition into Upper Nubia in the eighteenth regnal year of Senwosret I. Although the text is badly mutilated, it describes warlike activity: tents set on fire and grain hurled into the Nile. On the stela the god Mentu is shown presenting Senwosret I with a line of bound captives inscribed with names of Nubian peoples and places. The latter include Ashmeik and Sai Island. At the head of the list is Kush, which hereafter features prominently in Nubian history. Senwosret may have been accompanied on this campaign by Ameni, who later became Prince of the Oryx nome and one of the most powerful men in Middle Egypt. In his tomb, Ameni recounts that, while his father was still alive, he and his soldiers had accompanied Senwosret I when the king overthrew his enemies in Kush. Ameni claimed to have travelled south of Kush to the 'borders of the earth' and to have returned bearing tribute for the king.[8]

By the end of the Middle Kingdom, Kush was the name of a political entity that had its capital at Kerma, a short distance above the Third Cataract. We have already suggested that this region was the location of Iam, the country visited by Harkhuf during the Old Kingdom. It is unclear why the name Kush supplanted Iam in general usage, especially since the latter name also survived into later times. Posener has hypo-thesized that Kush was originally the name applied to the Nile Valley just up-river from Semna; eventually, however, the Egyptians extended this term to denote the important chiefdom farther to the south.[9] Sen-wosret I's name has been found on an offering stone as far up-river as Argo Island, a short distance south of Kerma.[10]

Senwosret I may have hoped to conquer the chiefdom of Kush and force it to pay him tribute. Such an arrangement would have given him control over Egypt's principal source of African products. Levying tribute would have cut the cost to the central government of obtaining these luxury goods and allowed the royal exchequer to determine more completely the volume and timing of deliveries. The ability to distribute more such commodities among the king's supporters would also have enhanced the prestige of the new dynasty. Alternatively, Senwosret I may have sought only to re-establish contact with the south and to ensure the safety of the trade routes through the Batn el-Hagar, perhaps doing no more than to repeat the exploits of Sneferu or other rulers of the Old Kingdom. It does not appear that either Senwosret I or any other Pharaoh of the Twelfth Dynasty held lasting suzerainty over Kush.

In the reign of Senwosret I, the Egyptians began to exploit the natural resources of Lower Nubia far more intensively than ever before. There is no evidence that gold was mined in Lower Nubia during the Old Kingdom, when most of the gold used by the Egyptians came from

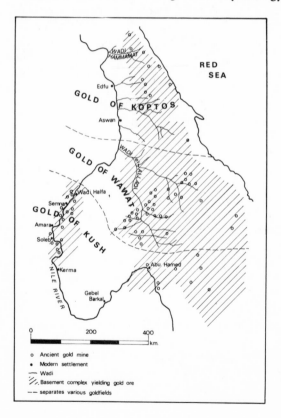

Fig.17 Ancient gold mines of Egypt and Nubia after Vercoutter 1959: map 2)

the Eastern Desert adjacent to Upper Egypt. Under Senwosret I the Egyptians began to mine for gold in the Wadi el-Allaqi and its main tributary the Wadi Gabgaba.[11] A copper mine at Abu Seyal, in the same region, also appears to have been worked at this time. The slag heaps and furnaces at Abu Seyal indicate that some smelting was done at the mine.[12] The fortress of Quban, at the mouth of the Wadi el-Allaqi, served as the control point for mining operations in the desert hinterland. Most of the gold from the Eastern Desert was smelted and stored for shipment there. Scales and weights used for weighing gold were found in the forts at Semna and Uronarti. They suggest that the Egyptians were also extracting the gold that occurs in the rock along the Nile between Wadi Halfa and Dongola.[13]

Fig. 17

THE CAMPAIGNS OF SENWOSRET III

While Senwosret I's successor, Amenemhet II, continued to exploit Lower Nubia, he does not appear to have made any effort to extend his power southward. It was the latter's grandson Khakaure-Senwosret III (1878–1843 B C) who gave definitive expression to the Middle Kingdom regime in Lower Nubia and who centuries later was to be worshipped as a patron deity throughout the region. Senwosret III was a vigorous ruler who sought to increase royal control in every sphere. His reign saw the disappearance of the provincial nobility that had played a prominent role within Egypt since the Sixth Dynasty and a correspond-ing increase in the power of the king.[14]

Plate 16

Early in his reign, Senwosret III had a canal called 'Beautiful are the Ways of Khakaure' cut near the island of Sehel in the First Cataract. This canal was about 80 metres long and was constructed primarily for the use of his warships. A similar attempt to facilitate riverine transport had been carried out by the official Weni early in the Sixth Dynasty.[15] In the king's eighth regnal year the canal was dredged and the fort at Aswan was strengthened. Following this, Senwosret began the first of his campaigns 'to overthrow defeated Kush'.[16] It is unclear how far south his army penetrated; however a stela set up at Semna at the conclusion of this campaign records the king's decision to make the Semna Cataract his southern frontier.[17] The location was well chosen, being the most constricted passage along the entire course of the Nile and impassable by boat at some times of the year.

Plate 17

There are references to additional campaigns against Kush in the tenth, twelfth, sixteenth, and possibly nineteenth regnal years of Senwosret III. A water level recorded at the Dal Cataract, 60 kilometres south of Semna, dates from the tenth year of his reign.[18] One purpose of these campaigns may have been to seize control of gold workings as far south as the Third Cataract, although Senwosret III's larger ambition may have been to conquer the chiefdom of Kush. Yet, while ships were employed in these expeditions, mention of wells as a military objective suggests that at least in part they were directed against nomadic tribes living east of the Nile rather than against the ruler of Kush. Senwosret III may have come to regard an intimidated ruler of Kush as a valuable trading partner and the principal objective of his later campaigns been to protect the trade routes beyond Semna. The gold and one or more female slaves that an official records bringing from Kush in his reign may have been booty from such a raid.[19]

Senwosret III appears to have stuck by his early decision not to try to implant Egyptian sovereignty south of Semna. His plan was to fortify the border at this point so that movement from the south by land or by water could be controlled. At the same time, he encouraged Nubians from the south to come to the Second Cataract region to trade. His explicit requirement that all trading with the Egyptians be carried on at a fortress down-river from Semna ensured that as far as the Egyptians were concerned this trade would remain a royal monopoly. The region between Kerma and Semna was hazardous for travel and there were marauding tribes in the Eastern Desert. Because of this, it is unlikely that individuals or small groups of traders would have travelled north by themselves. More likely, regular flotillas were despatched by the ruler of Kush who in this way would have retained a *de facto* monopoly over trade with the north.

Fig. 18

In the reign of Senwosret III, the Middle Kingdom forts in Lower Nubia achieved their final form. This involved a massive building programme that saw the erection of new forts, such as Uronarti and perhaps the Upper Fort at Mirgissa, and the enlargement of other forts that had been built as early as the reign of Senwosret I.[20] These forts are among the most impressive monuments of the Middle Kingdom that have survived into modern times. Their geographical distribution and close similarities in design suggest that they were planned to function as

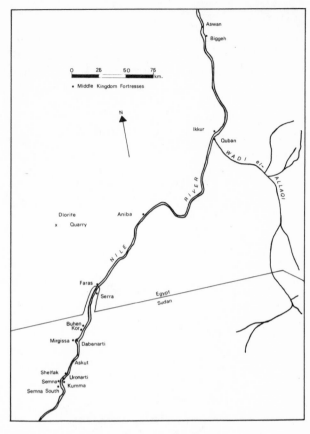

Fig. 18 Map of Egyptian fortresses in Lower Nubia during
the Middle Kingdom

a unit. Each fort was surrounded by a massive enclosure wall of mud
brick, strengthened with varying amounts of timber laid both parallel
to the face of the wall and at right angles to it. On rocky terrain, the
enclosure walls were irregular in outline and were provided with
massive spur walls dominating their location; on level ground they were
roughly rectangular. Where the natural setting did not suffice for protection, the enclosure walls, with their bastions, fortified gates, and draw-
bridges, were surrounded by a broad ditch protected by loopholed
ramparts on the inside and a glacis surmounted by a covered walkway
on the outside. These defences were carefully arranged so that archers
could direct a cross-fire that would cover all the approaches to the fort.
A space was also left free around the inside of the enclosure wall to

Fig. 19
Plate 18

69

facilitate its defence.[21] In their day, these forts must have been im-
pregnable and could have been defended by a small number of soldiers.
It has been suggested that their sophisticated design may have incorporated improvements that had been devised for forts that had been built
in Egypt during the First Intermediate Period, but of which few examples
have survived.[22]

The interiors of the forts were arranged on a grid plan. The streets,
which ran at right angles to the enclosure walls, were paved and provided with drains to carry off occasional heavy rains. Sections of the
fort were allocated for barracks, officers' houses, workshops, storerooms, and a governor's house that probably served as a royal residence
on the occasion of state visits. Any temples must have been of very
simple construction. While the interiors of the forts were originally laid
out with geometrical precision, this symmetry was quickly modified by

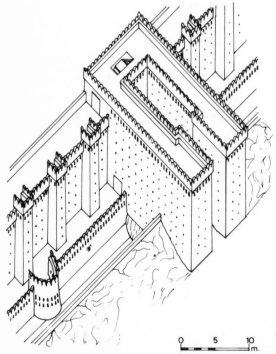

0   5   10
m.

*Fig. 19 Reconstruction of the West Gate
of the Middle Kingdom fortress at Buhen
(after Emery 1965 : fig. 10)*

rebuilding, which was adapted to individual needs rather than conforming to a general plan. All of the forts were located along the Nile and had
quays for unloading supplies as well as covered river-stairs that ensured
a supply of water during siege.

Plate 19

The amount of living space inside the forts suggests that the largest of
them did not have a garrison of more than 300 soldiers and their families;[23]
however, several thousand soldiers and support staff must have been
stationed in the thirteen or more forts that were occupied during the
Middle Kingdom; compared to an estimated C-Group population for
Lower Nubia of about 10,000.[24] It is generally assumed that all of
these soldiers came from Egypt, but Nubian recruits may have made up
part of the force.[25] The funerary stelae from Buhen indicate that many
of the Egyptians who were stationed at that fort came from the Theban
district. Thus they came from the part of Egypt that most resembled
Nubia and an area in which Nubians had long been settled.[26]

Most forts appear to have possessed a few cattle and small plots of
land that supplied dairy products and fresh vegetables for the garrison.
It is also possible that meat, dairy products, and grain were requisitioned
from the local population, although it is unlikely that sufficient surpluses
were produced in Lower Nubia to make this an important or reliable
source of provisions. Most food was probably despatched to the forts
from government warehouses in Egypt. This must have required
considerable organization and employed many ships and men full time.

In addition to guard duty and keeping watch over the adjacent
deserts, the men occupying the forts had to load and unload ships,
conduct donkey trains through the cataract region, and haul ships
around the rapids. On the desert plain north of Mirgissa, the French
Archaeological Mission found the remains of a mud slipway about
3 metres wide and 2 kilometres long that the Egyptians had used to drag
boats around the worst of the Kabuka Rapids. The prints of bare human
feet and of boat keels were visible in the dried mud.[27] The forts also
manufactured military equipment. In the armoury at Mirgissa, Vercoutter excavated stone lasts on which hide shields had been stretched
and shaped. The stone javelin points and crescent-shaped arrowheads
found there were also probably produced locally, using stone imported
from Egypt.[28] It is unknown whether the shields were manufactured
only for local use or if surplus ones went to supply the army in Egypt.

Plate 20

Plate 21

Besides the soldiers, boatmen, construction workers, and quarrymen must have constituted a sizable floating population travelling between Egypt and Nubia.

Five forts were built within sight and signalling distance of one another to command Egypt's southern frontier. The largest and most important of these forts was an L-shaped structure that a late Middle Kingdom papyrus informs us was called 'Khakaure (Senwosret III) is powerful'.[29] It was built on a rocky eminence on the west side of the Semna Rapids. Opposite it, on the east bank of the river and on what sometimes may have been an island, was the much smaller fortress of Kumma (called 'Warding off the Bows'). It too was built on a rocky eminence. These two forts commanded the river and could block any movement northward along the shore. Semna South ('Subduer of Nubia'), a large rectangular enclosure on the west bank about a kilo-metre south of Semna, seems to have been used in connection with military expeditions and for preparing trading convoys from the south for the overland journey to Mirgissa.[30] Uronarti ('Repelling the Inu') was a fort of modest dimensions built on a rocky island just north of Semna, while Shelfak ('Curbing the Countries') was a still smaller one atop a high nearby hill along the west bank. Farther north, in the lonely region between Shelfak and Mirgissa, there was at least one other fort, on the island of Askut.[31] Also apparently of Middle Kingdom date was a fortified brick wall over 4.5 kilometres long, which ran parallel to the east bank of the river between Semna and Uronarti.

Mirgissa, which is on the west bank of the Nile at the head of the formidable Kabuka Rapids, was the largest of the Nubian forts. The Upper Fort, which was located on a high eminence overlooking the Nile, was a large rectangular structure with a double retaining wall on the three landward sides. Along the river to the north was a sprawling, partially fortified settlement equipped with extensive port facilities. This appears to have been a large trading settlement. Vercoutter has provision-ally dated the founding of the lower town to the reign of Senwosret I and the construction of the Upper Fort to Senwosret III. Mirgissa is identified as being the fortress of Iken that was the prescribed destination of all Nubians who were allowed to pass north of Semna to trade or meet with Egyptian officials.[32] Mirgissa was thus the principal entrepot for trading with Kush and its size reflects the importance of this trade.

Plate 22;
Fig. 20a

Plate 23;
Fig. 20b

Plate 24
Fig. 20c

Fig. 21
Plates 25, 26;
Fig. 20d

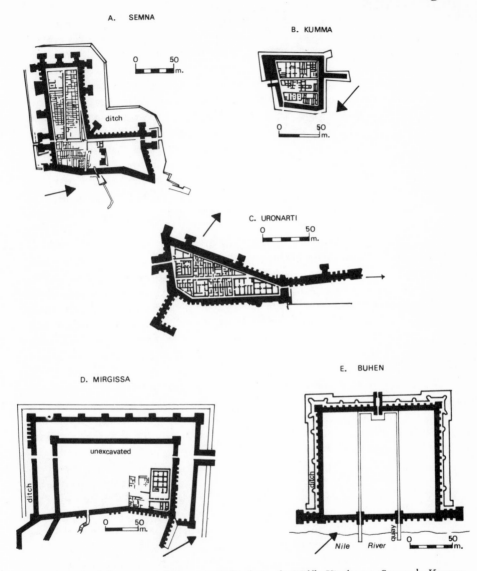

Fig. 20 Plans of five Egyptian fortresses in Nubia during the Middle Kingdom: a Semna; b Kumma; c Uronarti; d Mirgissa (Upper Fort); e Buhen (after Emery 1965: figs 19–24)

Fig. 20e

The small fort of Dabenarti on an island opposite Mirgissa may never have been finished or occupied.[33] This may be because, following the securing of the Semna frontier, the defence of more northerly stretches of the river became less important. The northernmost of the Cataract Forts was Buhen, located just south of the long-abandoned Egyptian Old Kingdom settlement. This fort was of considerable administrative importance and being located just below the Second Cataract was the key link between the Cataract Forts and Egypt. By the reign of Sen-wosret III the settlement at Kor, close to Buhen, had doubled in size and stretched for about 900 metres along the river. The growth of this settlement also seems to indicate the increasing economic as distinct from military importance of the Cataract region. Between Kor and Mirgissa is the island fortress of Dorginarti which may or may not date from the Middle Kingdom.

The Cataract Forts to the north of Shelfak were linked by a series of lookouts and signalling posts. These were all located west of the Nile and were manned by relays of soldiers sent out from neighbouring forts. One important lookout was atop the Rock of Abu Sir, which dominated the Second Cataract. Its signal fire was visible from both Buhen and Mirgissa. On the plain to the north, lookouts were located atop isolated desert buttes. While some of the sentry posts could have given the forts advance notice of the arrival of merchant ships or donkey caravans, others can only have been used to watch for enemies who might try to circumvent the Egyptian fortresses by travelling through the desert.[34]

The Cataract Forts were an important link in a trading network that secured prized luxury goods for the Egyptian state. All of the forts with the possible exception of Kumma were located either on the west bank of the river or on islands. Yet the adjacent Western Desert appears to have supported no significant nomadic population at this time while the east bank, which was the home of the Medjay, was left unfortified. This suggests that the Egyptians had little interest in building forts to curb the Medjay in this region even though we know from texts that the Egyptians kept watch over the latter's movements. Nor could the local C-Group alone have posed a threat requiring such elaborate defences.

Nevertheless it is difficult to accept Adams' suggestion that these forts were merely another example of the 'material hypertrophy which is typical of Egyptian civilization', in other words, glorified customs posts.[35] Early in the Twelfth Dynasty the Egyptians had penetrated beyond Kerma, which was probably the centre of the Kushite state. It is not known whether they were seeking to annex Kush or to eliminate mutual enemies who were interfering with trade routes. Yet, despite the profitable and apparently amicable trading relationship that developed, the strength of the Kushite state may have caused the Egyptians to fear that the fleet that brought trade goods north to Iken might some day bring a Kushite army. They may also have feared that a Kushite ruler might try to sow disaffection among the C-Group of Lower Nubia and tempt them to rally to his colours. Thus a well defended border probably seemed to be the best way of ensuring the safety of Lower Nubia. In view of the marked concern that the Pharaohs of the Middle Kingdom exhibited for protecting all of Egypt's frontiers, it was not out of character for them to have reacted energetically to the threat that they believed was posed by a powerful polity in northern Dongola. This cautious attitude may also explain why the ruler of Kush was listed among the enemies or potential enemies of the Pharaoh in the 'Execration Texts' of the late Middle Kingdom. The purpose of these texts was magically to counter-act the power of the Pharaoh's enemies.[36]

An ambivalent attitude towards the Nubians is also expressed in the 'Victory Stelae' that Senwosret III erected at Semna and Uronarti in his sixteenth regnal year. On these stelae, Senwosret boasts of the weak-ness of his Nubian foes and of his victories in the south. Posterity is warned, however, that while the Nubians will withdraw in the face of a strong and determined adversary they will be quick to take advantage of any weakness on the part of the Egyptians. Senwosret's heirs are urged to remain vigilant and to maintain the Semna boundary if they wish to validate themselves as rulers of Egypt.[37]

North of the Cataract zone, the Egyptians constructed a series of widely separated forts, most of which appear to have been concerned with the protection and provisioning of river traffic. The first of these forts was located at Serra, on the steeply sloping east bank of the river. This fort contained a basin that allowed ships to dock within its walls.[38] Its name 'Repressing the Medjay' suggests that one of its functions was to guard the adjacent stretch of shoreline against attacks by pastoralists from the Eastern Desert. A small fort equipped with a stone quay was

Plate 27

Plate 28

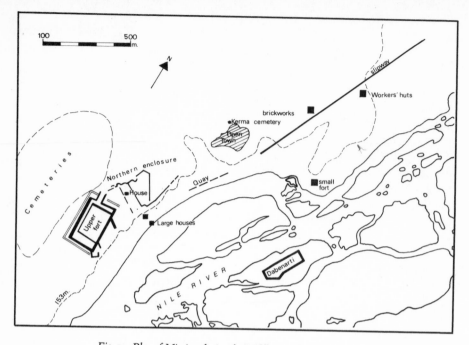

Fig. 21 Plan of Mirgissa during the Middle Kingdom and the Second Intermediate Period (after Vercoutter 1970 : fig. 4)

found alongside the now dried-up west channel of the Nile opposite the former Island of Faras. This fort was probably called Ink-towe ('Embracing the Two Lands').[39] Farther north there was a large rectangular fort on the west bank of the Nile at Aniba and another at Ikkur. Built on level ground, these forts dominated the principal fertile plains in Lower Nubia, which were also major centres of C-Group population. The forts as well as the districts in which they were located were called Miam and Baki respectively. The strong landward defences of these forts suggest that they were concerned less with con-trolling surrounding territory than with securing the safety of the river.

A few kilometres south of Ikkur, on the east bank of the river, was the fortress of Quban which, as we have already noted, was associated with mining operations in the Wadi el-Allaqi. These mining opera-tions probably required military protection to ward off interference by the Medjay. Egyptian texts list two other forts, at Bigeh and Aswan. These served as control points for transporting goods past the First

Cataract and for the protection and exploitation of the Aswan quarries.

No more evidence of fortifications was found at Toshka West for the Middle Kingdom than for the Old Kingdom. Presumably this was because there was little if any nomadic population to hinder Egyptian operations in the Western Desert at either period. Two sandstone stelae indicate that there must have been a depot at Toshka for provision‚ ing the expeditions to the diorite quarries. The longer of the inscriptions records that, in the fourth year of Amenemhet II, the reporter Horemhet came to fetch stone. He was accompanied by a work force made up of guardsmen, officials, lapidaries, quarry experts, workmen, and over 1000 donkeys.[40]

Plate 29

THE C‚GROUP UNDER EGYPTIAN OCCUPATION

Egyptian raids, and the elimination of the Nubians' control of Nile Valley trade, are assumed to account for the disappearance of the A‚Group. Unlike the Terminal A‚Group, the C‚Group people do not appear to have become heavily dependent on food imported from Egypt during the First Intermediate Period; hence they were not disrupted by the reassertion of Egyptian domination in the Middle Kingdom. Moreover, the moderate policies by which the early Pharaohs of the Twelfth Dynasty established their authority in Egypt probably inclined them to attain their ends in Nubia in as gentle a manner as possible. Chief among their purposes was once again to enjoy a monopoly over trade with Kush. Thus they did not seek to control Lower Nubia by exterminating, driving out, or deporting its native inhabitants. Instead, they established a series of forts to protect their frontiers and lines of communication and to allow them to facilitate their exploitation of the Eastern Desert.

It appears that Bietak's C‚Group Ib culture lasted well into the period of Egyptian occupation before it evolved into his IIa culture. In phase IIa the superstructures of graves were broader and lower than before. Grave pits were mostly rectangular and sometimes were lined and covered with large stone slabs. Bodies were generally flexed on their right side facing north or west. Hemispherical bowls continued to be made of black‚topped and black‚incised wares, although some of the bowls now had flattened bottoms. Globular redware pots were added to the repertoire of native vessels. These were often incised with geo‚

metrical or naturalistic designs around the shoulder. Pottery figurines representing women and cattle were also buried with the dead.[41]

Most C-Group settlements of the Middle Kingdom consisted of houses partly built of dry stone walls. In level II of the stratified Nubian village site at Aniba, the German excavators discovered a settlement dating from the Middle Kingdom. It contained semi-subterranean houses, the lower parts of which were formed of upright stone slabs chinked with mud and smaller stones. Two types of dwelling were present: single-room circular structures and agglomerations of curvilinear rooms. In the circular houses, the roof was supported by a complex structure of beams that eliminated the need for a centre pole and the entrance was through a small anteroom that cut off a direct view into the

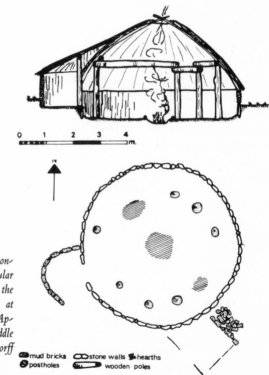

Fig. 22 Plan and reconstructed section of circular house from level II of the C-Group village at Aniba, Lower Nubia. Approximately time of Middle Kingdom (after Steindorff 1937)

mud bricks   stone walls   hearths
postholes   wooden poles

interior. One of these houses was 6 metres in diameter and enclosed   *Fig. 22*
three hearths arranged in a straight line. Hence not all of the circular
structures were granaries.[42] The agglomerated houses were up to 17
metres long and contained as many as eight rooms. Silos and tethering
posts for domestic animals were found within these houses. Similar
house types occur elsewhere in Lower Nubia. Villages do not appear to
have been large. House units were arranged in no particular order and
often were located some distance from one another. Both the round and
agglomerated houses appear to have been inhabited by extended families.

No unusually large or elaborately built houses have been found that
could be interpreted as the residences of chiefs; nor are there any obvious
shrines or temples. While some graves are more elaborate than others,
there is no distinct cleavage between rich and poor ones and no special
cemeteries or parts of cemeteries were reserved for the interment of
people of high status. This suggests that the C-Group remained an
egalitarian, tribal society in which status differences were not expressed
in terms of a distinct lifestyle. It is not surprising that more differences can
be observed among graves than among houses, since it is normal in
tribal societies for status to be reflected more in honours accorded to the
dead than in privileges claimed by the living.[43]

No fundamental restructuring of C-Group society can be correlated
with the Twelfth Dynasty occupation of Lower Nubia. Some Nubians
were made to wash gold and all of them may have had to pay taxes
in kind, although there is no solid evidence for this.[44] Given the small
amount of grazing land in Lower Nubia, it is unlikely that a cattle
tax was of any economic importance to Egypt.[45] On the whole, the
C-Group do not appear to have been severely exploited by the Egyptians
and the archaeological evidence indicates no reluctance on their part to
settle near the Egyptian forts.

The amount of Egyptian goods in C-Group cemeteries had begun to
decline already in the Eleventh Dynasty as a result of the restoration of a
state managed economy and a slackening demand for foreign mercenaries
in Egypt. The dearth of such goods in graves dating from the Middle
Kingdom suggests the absence of close economic or social ties between
the occupants of the Egyptian forts and the C-Group. Most of the
Nubians' clothing was made of locally produced leather; according to
the evidence of burials, men wore a kilt, sandals, and a cap. Cloth is

normally found only as a wrapping for occasional copper mirrors. Stone adzes were common and most jewellery was locally made from shell, bone, or stone; the shells occasionally coming from as far away as the Red Sea. Egyptian faience beads were not uncommon but metal objects, and especially metal weapons, occur rarely. A paucity of Egyptian pottery vessels also indicates that less food was being obtained from the Egyptians than in the First Intermediate Period.[46]

Nevertheless, the C-Group benefited from an imposed intertribal peace and from the protection that the Egyptians offered them against raids from the Eastern Desert. There appears to have been a significant increase in the number of archaeological sites at this time.[47] There also appears to have been a real though not spectacular increase in prosperity. Modest improvements in the complexity of C-Group culture, as witnessed by the elaboration of pottery and burial types during the Middle Kingdom, suggest an economy that was able to provide more rather than less for each individual than had been the case previously. The construction of more elaborate houses may also indicate less seasonal movement than in the past as well as a greater sense of security.

The increasing C-Group population must have depended on expanded agricultural production. Yet whatever increase was achieved by the C-Group occurred within the limitations of floodplain cultivation. Soils requiring any form of irrigation were still being avoided and the overall distribution of sites at this period closely resembles that of the A-Group. Possibly there were fewer sites in the far north, but the same concentrations of sites in the Dakka, Aniba, and Faras areas can be observed for the two cultures.[48] The large cemeteries in the major centres also indicate the longevity of these communities.

The Egyptian occupation of Lower Nubia would surely have increased the affluence and prestige of headmen who lived close to the fortresses, had the Egyptians chosen to employ such men to mediate relations between the C-Group and the occupying forces. That this sort of headman cannot be recognized in the archaeological record accords with the general lack of evidence of significant interaction between the Egyptians and the C-Group. On the contrary, the Egyptian occupation appears to have inhibited the development of marked economic and social differences within the C-Group. While the population increased, they remained an egalitarian, tribal society cut off from Egyptian influences rather than exposed to them. In this respect, the C-Group of the Middle Kingdom stands in marked contrast to the Classic and Terminal A-Group people who had intimate commercial ties with Upper Egypt. If one purpose of the Cataract Forts was to eliminate contact between the C-Group and politically more developed societies to the south, this stultification may have been the result of deliberate Egyptian policy.

CHAPTER VI

The Kerma Ascendancy

THE END OF THE MIDDLE KINGDOM

During the early part of the Middle Kingdom, Nile water levels appear to have been approximately the same as in recent times. The water stairs of Middle Kingdom forts descend to present low-water, while high-water docking facilities at Mirgissa and elsewhere are at the same level as modern ones. Evidence suggests, however, that there may have been greater variability than at present in Nile levels during the late winter.[1]

Plate 30

It is clear that there was a succession of extraordinarily high Nile floods between 1840 and 1770 BC. Many annual high-water marks are recorded in a series of inscriptions that were carved on both banks of the Nile above the Semna Cataract. Most of these inscriptions date from the reign of Amenemhet III, but there are others from the reigns of Amenemhet IV and Queen Sobeknefru, the last ruler of the Twelfth Dynasty, and Sekhemre-Khutowe and Sekhemkare, the first kings of the Thirteenth Dynasty. These inscriptions record floods that are on an average 8 metres higher than those of modern times. While it was once believed that the difference could be accounted for in terms of subsequent erosion of the Semna Cataract, it has been necessary to discard this interpretation. Apart from the adverse geological arguments, an inscription at Askut, downstream from Semna, records a similar high-water level in the third regnal year of Sekhemkare.[2]

Fig. 23

These high floods damaged Egyptian installations in Nubia. The glacis of the fort at Semna South was overwhelmed by a silt deposit over 8 metres deep, laid down in the waters impounded behind the Semna Cataract.[3] Ancient fields 6 to 7 metres above present high-water level at Shelfak and Uronarti probably date from this period, while the foundations of the fort at Dabenarti, which is located in a less constricted portion of the valley, are waterworn 5 metres above present high-water. At Mirgissa the lower town was severely flood damaged up to 6 metres above what had been the high-water level earlier in the Middle Kingdom. It is also possible that the harbour at Serra East was silted up at this time

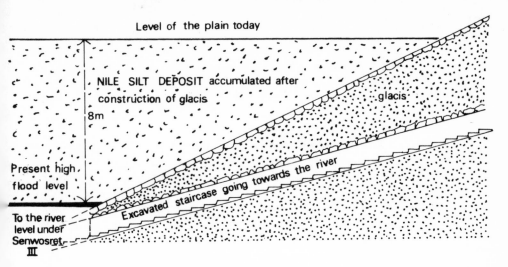

Level of the plain today

NILE SILT DEPOSIT accumulated after construction of glacis

glacis

8m

Present high flood level

Excavated staircase going towards the river

To the river level under Senwosret III

Fig. 23 Cross-section of the lower end of the glacis at Semna South (after Vercoutter 1966: fig. 4)

and that the protective stone footings around some of the forts farther north had to be strengthened.[4] There is no archaeological evidence that either these extraordinarily high floods or their subsequent recession adversely affected the native inhabitants of Lower Nubia. Likewise, under a strong central government, the Egyptians seem to have adjusted to this cycle of ecological changes; indeed, the reign of Amenemhet III was probably the most prosperous period of the Middle Kingdom.

It was once thought that following the end of the Twelfth Dynasty, *c.* 1786 BC, Egypt suffered a political collapse similar to that experienced at the end of the Sixth Dynasty. It now appears that for over a century the authority of the central government persisted, in spite of the rapid pace at which kings succeeded one another. The standards of Twelfth Dynasty court art were maintained and royal building activities were undertaken in various parts of Egypt. Yet it was not long before the town of Xois became the capital of a secessionist state that was to endure until 1603 BC in the swamplands of the western Delta. By 1720, Avaris, in the eastern Delta, was occupied by the Hyksos, rulers of Asiatic origin whose rise to power in Egypt is still highly controversial. By *c.* 1674, under King Salitis, the Hyksos were able to occupy the Middle Kingdom capital, Itj-towe. The Thirteenth Dynasty continued until 1633, apparently in the persons of Upper Egyptian princes who latterly were subordinate to the Theban rulers of the Seventeenth Dynasty. The latter were to reunite Egypt *c.* 1575 BC, thereby bringing to an end the Second Intermediate Period.[5]

THE RETREAT FROM LOWER NUBIA

Although there are no references to major Egyptian activities in Nubia after the reign of Senwosret III, the garrisons in Lower Nubia seem to have been maintained in good order until well into the Thirteenth Dynasty. While the Semna high-water records stop early in the Thirteenth Dynasty this apparently resulted from the cessation of ultra high floods rather than from any weakening of Egyptian control. A steatite plaque bearing the name of King Khasekhemre-Neferhotep (1740–1730 BC) has been found at Buhen and a rock inscription appears to attest his visit to the First Cataract. A statue of his brother and successor, Khaneferre-Sobekhotep that was found on Argo Island may have been carried there during the Second Intermediate Period from one of the Second Cataract forts.[6] It is possible, however, that a military expedition pushed as far south as Sai Island late in the Middle Kingdom.[7] The power of the Egyptian central government extended at least to Semna until *c.* 1720. Surviving despatches sent from Semna to the vizier in charge of the Far-South region of Egypt early in the Thirteenth Dynasty indicate that a careful watch was being kept on the pastoralists of the Eastern Desert, who sought assistance at Semna in times of drought.[8]

After 1720, the forts south of Aswan suffered from varying degrees of unchecked dilapidation, although there is evidence for the sporadic or continuous occupation of some of them. According to Emery, Buhen remained 'a more or less gigantic ruin until the reconquest of Nubia' in the Eighteenth Dynasty.[9] Some forts, such as Buhen, also appear to have been burned during the Second Intermediate Period. Arkell has argued that the C-Group continued to resent the Egyptian occupation throughout the Middle Kingdom and took advantage of Egyptian weakness to destroy their strongholds.[10] Emery suggested that it was the Kushites who captured these forts and set fire to them.[11] Adams points out that the evidence is insufficient to prove that any of these forts was taken by storm and he doubts that they could have been unless most of their garrisons had already been withdrawn. Some fires may have been set deliberately by the retreating Egyptians.[12]

It is possible that the Egyptian garrisons in Nubia were recalled to help the Egyptian government cope with the onslaught of the Hyksos. Alternatively, the waning power of the Thirteenth Dynasty may have left these garrisons to fend for themselves. Without regular supplies from Egypt, it would have been impossible for these forts to operate normally. Many soldiers may have chosen to return to Egypt, while others con/ tinued to live in or near the abandoned forts perhaps engaging, when circumstances allowed, in the trade that went on between Kush and Egypt. This remnant population may account for the considerable number of 'Egyptian graves' that have been attributed to the Second Intermediate Period in Lower Nubia. These led Reisner to believe that the country had been overrun by a wave of Egyptian settlers seeking refuge from Hyksos domination.[13] It may be descendants of these soldiers who were the Egyptians living at Buhen late in the Second Intermediate Period. It may also be through their intermarriage and closer commercial contacts with the indigenous people, that Egyptian customs were increasingly to influence the C/Group.

KERMA

The decline of Egyptian power in Lower Nubia correlates with the growing influence of Kush, whose capital during this period was almost certainly at Kerma. About 2 kilometres east of the Nile, on the edge of the Kerma Basin, Reisner excavated the Western Deffufa (a Nubian term for any prominent brick ruin). This was an almost solid mud brick structure 52 metres long, 26 metres wide, and still standing 19 metres high. Inside this structure, was a narrow stairway evidently leading to a platform at the top. Two additions had later been built against the east face of the building; one of which contained two small rooms entered at ground level and two vertical shafts with no horizontal openings. The brickwork and timber bonding was clearly Egyptian in character and closely resembles that of the Middle Kingdom forts. Around the base of the Deffufa was a warren of rectangular brick rooms. These rooms appear to have been rebuilt several times and some ante/dated the Deffufa. They contained stone and pottery vessels of Egyptian origin as well as raw materials and unfinished products

Fig. 24
Plate 31;
Fig. 25

85

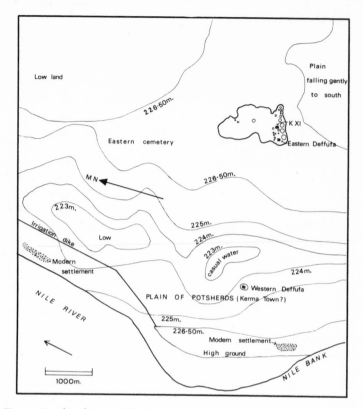

Fig. 24 Site plan of Kerma (after Reisner 1923a)

which indicated that pottery, faience, mica ornaments, and beads of
glazed quartzite, carnelian, and ostrich shell had been manufactured
there. Over 565 seal impressions were recovered that apparently had
been affixed to containers arriving from Egypt. Some of these sealings
bore the names of Mayebre Sheshi and Yakubher, the first two rulers of
the Fifteenth or 'Great Hyksos' Dynasty. Reisner notes that around the
Deffufa complex there were widespread traces of occupation, although
no remains of identifiable structures were located elsewhere. The
Deffufa was probably located in the centre of a sprawling town consisting mostly of reed houses and windscreens.[14]

Reisner interpreted the Western Deffufa as the fortified residence of an
Egyptian 'Governor General' of Upper Nubia in the Middle Kingdom.

Junker objected that at most it could have held fifty to one hundred men, that it had no source of water to withstand a siege, and that it was separated from the nearest large Egyptian fort by a great distance.[15] As the essentially non-military nature of the Deffufa was acknowledged, it became fashionable to describe it as an Egyptian trading post, established under the protection of the King of Kush. Even more recently it has been suggested that the Deffufa was not Egyptian at all but part of the palace of the King of Kush. Its construction may have been supervised by Egyptian craftsmen, who are known to have been employed by the Kushite rulers late in the Second Intermediate Period.[16]

Much that was produced at Kerma was heavily influenced by Egyptian techniques of manufacture and design and has been interpreted by Reisner and others as local manifestations of Egyptian culture. The upper classes at Kerma greatly admired Egyptian culture and had manufactured for their own use acceptable imitations of Egyptian furniture, jewellery, weapons, and even architecture. Yet much that was manufactured at Kerma belongs to an indigenous cultural tradition. Their coarse utility ware and the polished black bowls with white-filled decoration have much in common with the C-Group pottery of Lower Nubia. The most common luxury ware was an elegant black-topped pottery with a lustrous finish, extremely thin walls, and sharp rims. The lower exterior of this 'Kerma Ware' was deep red and was generally separated from the black upper part by an irregular strip that was metallic white in colour. Kerma Ware occurs in a wide variety of designs including open bowls, tulip-shaped beakers, and elegantly spouted vessels. It was so carefully made that Reisner wrongly concluded that it was shaped on a potter's wheel.[17] Pottery of this sort was produced in vast quantities and appears to have been prized elsewhere, sometimes occurring in non-Kerma graves in Lower Nubia and Egypt. Copper vessels duplicate the shapes of the local pottery and the copper daggers, of which over 130 were found at Kerma, are distinct local variants of standard Egyptian ones. While the design and carpentry of beds are typically Egyptian, the footboards were inlaid with ivory in what appears to be a local style. Likewise, many of the mica figures that were sewn onto caps are clearly not Egyptian in design.[18] Although many of these items have been interpreted as products of Egyptian craftsmen accommodating themselves to local tastes, it is equally possible that local

Plate 32;
Fig. 26

Plate 33

Plate 34

Fig. 27

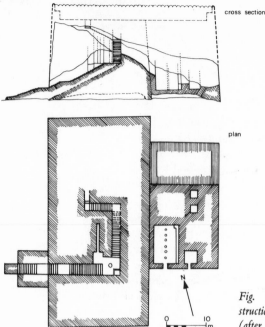

cross section

plan

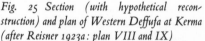

N

0   10
└─────┘ m.

Fig. 25 Section (with hypothetical recon-
struction) and plan of Western Deffufa at Kerma
(after Reisner 1923a: plan VIII and IX)

craftsmen acquired Egyptian techniques of manufacture and used them
to produce goods adapted to their own cultural idiom. No Egyptian
graves have been found at Kerma to indicate the presence of a sizable
colony of Egyptian artisans.

Adams has suggested that the Western Deffufa was an enormous
tower that permitted palace officials to watch the river for the arrival of
trading convoys.[19] The abundance of ivory at the site supports the
proposal that Kerma was the major collection point for raw materials
from the south and the entrepot from which these materials were sent
north through the Batn el-Hagar to be traded with the Egyptians. A
Kerma fleet may be represented by the boats depicted in the fragmentary
wall paintings that adorn the funerary chapels in the Kerma cemetery.
While much of the metal and faience goods that were manufactured
around the Western Deffufa was intended for the use of the court,
humbler items were probably made to be exchanged for raw materials
with tribesmen living to the south.

The most detailed information about Kerma society was recovered from the Eastern Cemetery, located on a low rise about 3 kilometres east of the Western Deffufa. This cemetery covers an area 1.5 kilometres long and 0.8 kilometres wide. Although only the southern edge of the cemetery has been systematically excavated, most graves consisted of oval or rectangular burial chambers dug into the hard subsoil and covered with low circular earth tumuli. Bodies were interred in a flexed position, on their right sides facing north. The principal burials rested on an angareeb or native Nubian bed, were covered with a hide, and supplied with a headrest and a pair of sandals. In addition to toilet articles and pottery vessels containing food and drink, slaughtered rams were buried with the dead and sometimes a row of ox skulls was arranged around the perimeter of the tumulus. Most of the larger graves in the southern part of the cemetery also contained one or more sacrificed human retainers.

Eight exceptionally large tumuli were located in a row along the southern edge of the cemetery. These ranged up to 90 metres in diameter and the largest were internally reinforced by a series of low mud brick walls running at right angles to a central corridor. Some of these mounds

Plate 35

Fig. 26 Kerma pottery: 1–12, 14 black-topped ware; 13 polished red ware; 15, 16, 17 black polished incised ware with white encrustations (after Emery 1965: fig. 31 and Reisner 1923b)

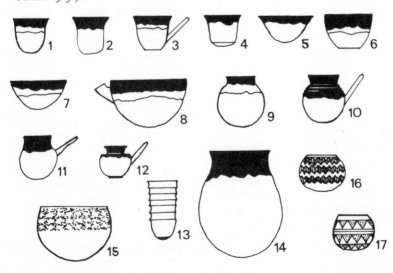

89

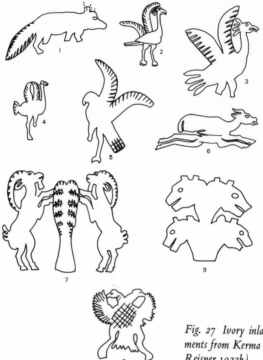

Fig. 27 Ivory inlays and mica cap ornaments from Kerma (after Junker 1932 and
Reisner 1923b)

Plate 36;
Fig. 28

Plate 37

were paved over with a mud brick skin and had a conical stone placed on their summit. Reisner believed that the largest tumulus (K III) was the oldest and dated it to the reign of Senwosret I. In this mound, he found part of a lifesize statue of Djefaihapi (Hepzifa), Prince of Assiut, and another complete one of his wife Sennuwy. Djefaihapi is known to have lived in the reign of Senwosret I. Reisner decided that Djefaihapi had come south as an Egyptian Governor and been buried at Kerma, largely in accordance with local rites. He also assumed that the highly developed arts and crafts evidenced in this tomb resulted from the recent arrival of skilled artisans from Egypt, whose skills degenerated as later tumuli were constructed.[20]

Säve-Söderbergh has demonstrated that tumulus K III cannot date from the reign of Senwosret I, since it also contained a lid inscribed with

90

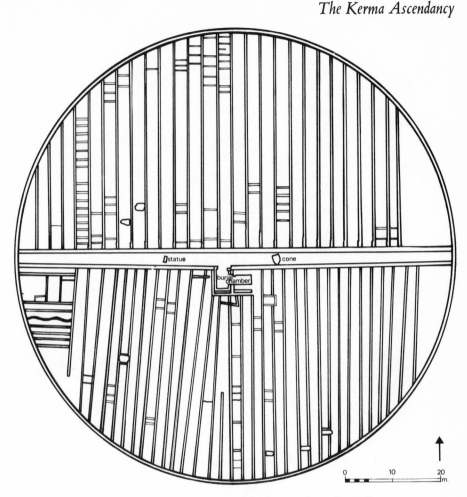

Fig. 28 K III, the largest of the royal tumuli at Kerma (after Reisner 1923a: plan XV)

the name of Amenemhet III and an ivory wand and scarabs dating
from the Second Intermediate Period.[21] It is now believed that many of
the statues of Egyptian kings and officials of the Middle Kingdom that
were found in K III and other tumuli were booty that the Kushites
carried off from Egyptian sites in Lower Nubia and possibly from
farther north. O'Connor has suggested that some of the large statues

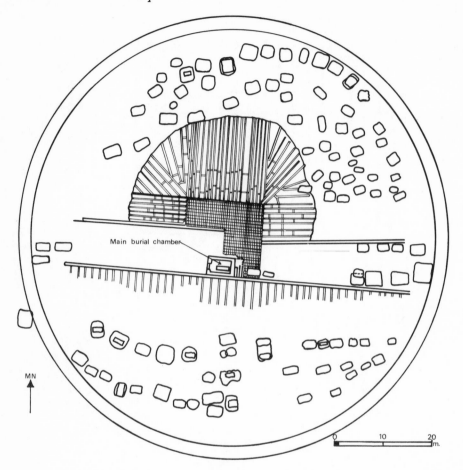

Main burial chamber

MN

0   10   20
m.

Fig. 29 K X, another of the large Kerma tumuli (after Reisner 1923a: plan XXI)

that appear to come from Middle Egypt (such as those of Djefaihapi and his wife) may have been gifts from Hyksos kings to their Kushite trading partners,[22] while other statues could have been traded by Egyptian merchants to the admiring rulers of Kerma. It seems likely that all of the great Kerma tumuli date from the Second Intermediate Period, that the largest of them were the latest, and that the standard of local crafts was improving rather than declining throughout this period.

Each of the large tumuli contained a mud brick burial chamber. In at least one of these, the body of the dead ruler was laid out on a bed made of glazed quartz; in another the bed was of slate. Although these chambers were all badly plundered, luxury goods, including model ships made from stone and faience, hint at the opulence of the interments. Beside the main burial chamber there was a large room, which in three tombs took the form of a central corridor traversing the diameter of the tumulus. These contained the skeletons of up to 400 human beings who had been buried alive in them. Their bodies were accompanied by few artefacts and many were of women who may have been part of the royal harem. The largest tumuli also contained as many as 100 subsidiary graves. These had been dug into the tumuli at various times subsequent to the principal interment. Most of them were rectangular pits, but in K III crosswalls were run between support walls within the tumulus to form small brick chambers. Each subsidiary

Plate 38
Plate 39

Fig. 29

Fig. 30 Mortuary Chapel K XI from the Eastern Cemetery at Kerma (Reisner 1923a: plan XIX)

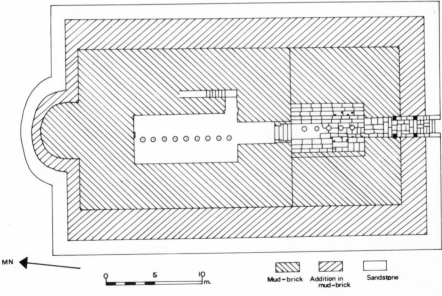

MN

Mud–brick	Addition in mud–brick	Sandstone

grave contained rich furnishings and a few human sacrifices. Around the main tumuli were 'minor' ones, nevertheless ranging to over 45 metres in diameter. It is likely that court officials who personally served the king were eventually interred in the same tumulus with him, while important members of the nobility and officials who were less close to the king were buried in their own adjacent tumuli.

Two massive mortuary chapels were associated with the royal tumuli. Both contained two long, narrow chambers that communicated by a single entrance to the outside. Although the brickwork was typically Egyptian, the single row of pillars running the length of each room is unparalleled in Egyptian architecture, which was dominated by a love of bilateral symmetry. Both structures may have had a second storey and *Fig. 30* one was faced with large blocks of sandstone. Fragments of a large cult statue were found in one of the chapels and the interiors of both were decorated with paintings showing human and animal activity. Although generally Egyptian in style, these scenes are distinctive in terms of themes and the arrangement of figures. Small square chambers, also believed to be funerary chapels, were found near the south sides of a few minor tumuli.

The great tumuli in the Kerma cemetery suggest a centralized monarchy, while many of the sacrificed retainers found in these and lesser graves were probably slaves. The occurrence of the latter in such large numbers suggests that warfare may have played an important role in Kerma's trading operations. It is significant, however, that the difference between the largest and humblest tombs is primarily one of scale and that, contrary to the practice in historic Egypt, tombs of all sizes are jumbled together in the same cemetery. Thus Adams is correct when he points out that, while there were marked differences in wealth and access to labour services among the freemen of Kerma, there is no evidence of sharply delineated social classes. Ties of kinship and earlier tribal associations may have remained strong; preventing full development of a class based society.[23]

Although the large tumuli along the southern edge of the Kerma cemetery date from the Second Intermediate Period, it is possible that the unpublished and largely unexcavated graves in the northern part of the cemetery are earlier. If so, this suggests that the power of the king and the development of the Kerma culture reached their apex late in the

Second Intermediate Period.[24] One indication of the growing power
and ostentation of the upper classes in the latter period is the increasing
incidence of retainer sacrifice both at Kerma and in less important
cemeteries. Although retainer sacrifice in high status burials had
apparently died out in Egypt by the end of the Early Dynastic Period,
it is evidenced in Nubia in Meroitic times and survived on a minor scale
among tribal groups in the Sudan until early in the present century. At
Kerma, the development of greater social complexity led, on the one
hand, to the elaboration of indigenous customs such as tumulus burials
and retainer sacrifice and, on the other, to the acquisition of a veneer of
Egyptian material culture by the Kerma elite.

Although little is known about the origin of the Kerma culture, it
appears to have developed from the A-Group or some closely related
culture in the Dongola area. Stylistically it is related to the C-Group
culture of Lower Nubia and is part of the C-Horizon described in the
last chapter. The Kerma culture is distinguished from other C-Horizon
cultures by its social complexity and by concomitant cultural elaboration and refinement. At present it is unknown how far south of Argo
Island the Kerma culture extended. To the north, the border between
the Kerma and C-Group cultures appears to have been at Semna.
The southernmost C-Group cemetery is reported from Saras, 14
kilometres north of Semna, while a number of Kerma cemeteries are
located just south of the Egyptian border forts.[25] What is not known is
whether an already existing ethnic frontier in the vicinity of Semna
helped to persuade Senwosret III to establish his southern boundary
there or whether the boundary itself was a factor promoting the differentia-
tion of the two cultures. A Kerma cemetery containing several hundred
graves has been excavated at Ukma in the Batn el-Hagar, while the
cemetery on Sai Island may be as large as the one at Kerma. There are
large tumuli in the Sai cemetery, although none are equal to the biggest
ones at Kerma. The graves and their contents are similar to the medium
range tumuli at Kerma except for the rarity of retainer sacrifices; which
may indicate that they antedate the southern graves at Kerma.[26]

The sealings bearing the names of Hyksos rulers that were found in
the rooms around the base of the Western Deffufa indicate that early in
the Fifteenth Dynasty extensive trade went on between Kush and Lower
Egypt.[27] The petty rulers of Upper Egypt apparently were unable to

interfere with this trade, which must have been of major importance to the Hyksos. The latter traded extensively with the countries of the eastern Mediterranean and ivory and ebony were no doubt among the products they exported. Nubia also may have traded gold to the Hyksos. While it is unlikely that the Kushites or the C-Group had the means to exploit the gold fields of the Wadi el-Allaqi, the Batn el-Hagar may have been of some importance as a producing area. The occurrence of various types of Near Eastern pottery at Kerma indicates that goods from these distant regions were making their way to Nubia for the first time.[28]

Monumental inscriptions bearing the names of the later Hyksos kings, Khyan and his successor Aweserre Apopi, have been found at Gebelein in Upper Egypt.[29] This suggests that they too were in a position to carry on trade with Kush and that the failure to find their sealings at Kerma is probably the result of chance. On the basis of historical evidence, it is unlikely that Kerma was abandoned in the later Hyksos period as the result of a Hyksos invasion.

LOWER NUBIA IN THE SECOND INTERMEDIATE PERIOD

There is no evidence that even a tenuous Hyksos sovereignty ever extended south of Aswan. The cessation of the Egyptian government's control of Lower Nubia, combined with the remoteness of the Hyksos and their lack of knowledge about the south, must have posed trading problems that the Kushites had not faced before. Such Egyptian troops as remained behind in Nubia were insufficent to maintain a large-scale flow of trade or to police the trade routes as they had done previously. Under these circumstances, the desire to maintain trade links with Egypt, far more than dynastic ambition, probably encouraged the Kushite rulers to expand their influence northward. While the Kushites may have extended their raids into Upper Egypt, the Theban king was in firm control of Aswan by the end of the Second Intermediate Period. Yet, at that time, everything south of Aswan appears to have been regarded as Kushite territory.[30]

At Mirgissa, Vercoutter excavated a Kerma cemetery and found that the Upper Fort had been occupied by what appears to have been a small band of Kushite pastoralists sometime between 1650 and 1580. No attempt had been made by them to maintain or repair the fort.[31]

Buhen similarly remained in ruins but there is evidence that it was inhabited late in the Second Intermediate Period by Kushites and by Egyptians who owed allegiance to the King of Kush. On a grave stela an Egyptian official named Sepedhor boasted that he was 'a valiant Commandant at Buhen' who 'built the temple of Horus, Lord of Buhen, to the satisfaction of the ruler of Kush'.[32] Honouring of the local deity is proof of Kushite control over Buhen. Another stela from Buhen records that an official named Ka was 'a capable servant of the ruler of Kush; who washed his feet in the waters of Kush in the retinue of the ruler Nedjeh and returned safely to his family'.[33] Ka evidently lived at Buhen and seems to have been recording a visit to Kerma on official business. Two small Kerma cemeteries were found at Saras East, north of Shelfak, and seven graves below the lookout at Abu Sir.[34] North of the Second Cataract a substantial number of Kerma burials were excavated at Aniba, while other graves have been found near the Egyptian forts at Quban, Ikkur, and Buhen, in C-Group cemeteries at Argin West, Debeira East, Faras East, Tomas, Mediq, Wadi el-Allaqi, and Dakka, and in Egypt as far north as Abydos.[35] While Kushites may have stationed small garrisons in the vicinity of the Second Cataract and in or near the Middle Kingdom fortresses farther north, they do not appear to have colonized Lower Nubia or attempted to hold the region by force. Many of the Kerma graves found near the fortresses appear to be those of prosperous traders or resident officials rather than of an occupying force. The Kushite monarch may have controlled Lower Nubia largely by striking alliances with its local inhabitants; both C-Group and Egyptian. Because of the importance of trade to the economy of this region, it was probably not difficult for the Kushites and these groups to conclude alliances grounded on mutual interest.

Although the Egyptian occupation of Lower Nubia officially may have ended suddenly, the archaeological record suggests that Egyptian influence waned gradually in the latter part of the Thirteenth Dynasty. The ebbing of Pharaonic power created new elements of risk for the C-Group, yet the Second Intermediate Period was a time of unprecedented prosperity for them. The population increased considerably and Egyptian trade goods were prevalent.[36] Presumably, the people of Lower Nubia were once more able to engage in trade or to charge tolls

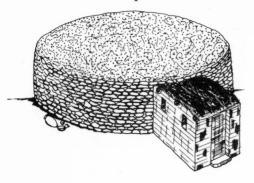

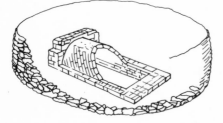

Fig. 31 A large C-Group grave with a barrel-vaulted mud brick burial chamber. Of the Second Intermediate Period (after Stein-dorff 1937)

on goods passing through their territory, a situation that apparently persisted even when the region was allied to Kerma or otherwise under its influence. Profits derived from this trade enhanced the status of local chiefs and perhaps of entrepreneurs, producing an indigenous society that economically and politically was considerably more complex than it had been formerly. Increasing prosperity also encouraged the Egyptian-ization of the C-Group, especially of the more prosperous and influential elements. This process was probably assisted by the resident Egyptians, who now traded and interacted with the Nubians far more intimately than they had done during the Middle Kingdom. At the same time, Kerma and Pan-Grave (Medjay) influences became noticeable, par-ticularly in funerary customs. This indicates that long suspended contacts with neighbouring peoples to the south and east had been resumed.[37]

C-Group graves of the Second Intermediate Period (Bietak's IIb period) varied in style and complexity far more than they did previously.

The superstructures continued to be constructed of stone blocks, but
large ones were now up to 16 metres in diameter and had rectangular
mud brick chapels on their east side. These large superstructures occur
only in small numbers on the margins of C-Group cemeteries and
appear to cover the graves of headmen. Bodies were interred in a semi-
flexed position on their right side, but now generally faced west rather
than north. In more elaborate burials, the body was placed in a crypt
built of rough stone slabs (as in the previous period) or in a small mud
brick chamber. The latter was roofed with wood, stone slabs, or an
Egyptian style mud brick vault. The vault normally projected above
ground level but was covered by the gravel fill of the superstructure.
Pottery was placed beside the corpse more frequently than before. An
occasional bed burial, as well as the growing frequency with which
gazelles, sheep, and other animals were placed in the grave, suggest
Kerma influence. Similarly, animal skulls painted with patterns in
red and black that occur among the offerings left in the grave-chapels

Fig. 31

Plate 40

Fig. 32

*Fig. 32 C-Group pottery
of the Second Intermediate
Period: 1–3 black incised
ware with encrusted colour;
4–5 rough decorated ware;
6 cylindrical vessel of hard
ware; 7 pottery stand; 8, 9
pottery figurines (after
Bietak 1968: pls 12, 13)*

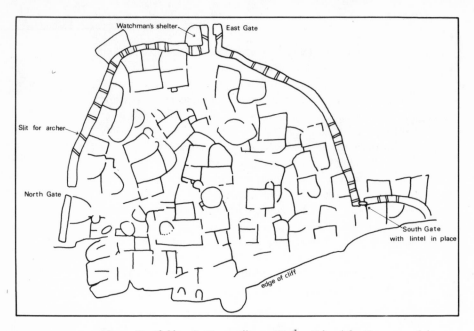

Fig. 33 Fortified late C-Group village at Wadi es-Sebua (after Sauneron 1965)

or around the perimeter of the superstructures indicate the borrowing of Pan-Grave customs. Copper and bronze daggers and axes were buried with the dead more frequently than during the Middle Kingdom, when their sale to the C-Group may have been curtailed. Most of these weapons of the late C-Group are of Egyptian rather than Kerma manufacture.[38] By contrast with the Kerma culture, there is no evidence of retainer sacrifice in connection with even the most important burials.

The trend towards larger and more substantial dwellings that was noted for the C-Group during the Middle Kingdom continued into the Second Intermediate Period. In some parts of Lower Nubia there is also evidence of a concern for defence that may reflect the breakdown of the *Pax Aegyptia*. At Wadi es-Sebua, over one hundred tightly clustered houses have been dated to the end of the Thirteenth Dynasty. Like earlier C-Group dwellings, the lower portions of these houses were constructed of upright stone slabs and they consisted of round single room dwellings and agglomerations of irregularly shaped rooms. The

Fig. 33

village was protected on the east side by a cliff falling to the river and on
the other sides by a semi-circular perimeter wall built of rough stone
blocks. This wall was pierced by three gates, the largest of which
was protected by a guardhouse and a spur wall. Thirty-two archers'
loopholes distributed along the perimeter wall appear to copy the
architecture of the Egyptian fortresses.[39]

Of equal architectural interest is the so-called 'Nubian castle' at
Amada. This was a settlement 80 metres long and 40 metres wide that
was inhabited from sometime in the Middle Kingdom into the middle of
the Eighteenth Dynasty. It was partially rebuilt at various intervals.
The original structure appears to have been a group of tightly clustered
C-Group houses surrounded by a roughly rectangular stone wall.

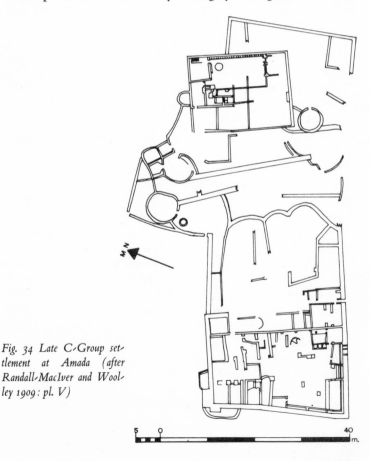

*Fig. 34 Late C-Group set-
tlement at Amada (after
Randall-MacIver and Wool-
ley 1909: pl. V)*

The Kerma Ascendancy

Fig. 34

Later, two rectangular buildings were erected at either end of the village with no evident concern for preserving the community's defences. The new structures were built mainly of mud brick. The western building had a courtyard with various small rooms disposed around it. The eastern unit was laid out on more formal and spacious principles. It contained one large rectangular room, with a bench designed to hold large pottery vessels running the length of the outer wall; this may have been a banqueting hall.[40] It is possible that the village at Amada was the seat of a Nubian chief who, either late in the Second Intermediate Period or in the New Kingdom, erected the two large buildings for his own use. A similar village was found near Karanog.[41] All of these fortified settlements may have been the headquarters of C-Group chiefs and are perhaps a sign of their growing power in the Second Intermediate Period.

There is further evidence of Egyptianizing trends in C-Group architecture late in the Second Intermediate Period and early in the New Kingdom. The upper level of the C-Group village at Aniba contained a number of rectangular brick structures each about $2\frac{1}{2}$ metres long.[42] At Debeira, the Scandinavian Joint Expedition excavated a rectangular brick house and an Egyptian cupola shaped granary next to a traditional C-Group house. Another house in that district contained late C-Group artefacts but was built entirely in an Egyptian fashion, with square rooms and mud brick walls laid on stone foundations.[43]

In the domestic arts, black-incised bowls were now encrusted with polychrome, as well as white, decoration and black-incised cups appeared for the first time. Large square ceramic tables and pot stands with decorative open-work sides may attest greater adaptation to sedentary life. Yet there is no evidence of a more specialized division of labour to match the increasing status differences attested in the C-Group cemeteries and settlements. There is also no evidence for the emergence of sharply differentiated classes during the Second Intermediate Period. In power and influence even the most important C-Group chiefs fell far short of the Kerma monarchs. The absence of retainer sacrifice suggests a dearth of slaves or perhaps the restraining influence of Egyptian customs. At its most developed, the C-Group was a modest and truncated reflection of Kushite society.

CHAPTER VII

The New Kingdom

THE REUNIFICATION OF EGYPT

About 1575 BC, the whole of Egypt was again brought under Theban hegemony. This marked the beginning of the New Kingdom, a third phase of vigorous national government that was to last for almost 500 years. The founders of the New Kingdom were descendants of princes who had regarded themselves as the rightful rulers of Egypt and as potential liberators of their country from alien usurpers. These self-styled monarchs of the Seventeenth Dynasty ruled over the southern part of Upper Egypt but prudently acknowledged Hyksos suzerainty until almost the end of the Second Intermediate Period. This suzerainty was formally rejected by the Pharaoh Sekenenre-Tao. His son, Kamose, continued to harass the aged Aweserre-Apopi and, before the end of Kamose's brief reign, the Thebans controlled the Nile Valley as far north as the entrance to the Fayum. Sekenenre's rebellion must have severed the profitable trade that had gone on between the Hyksos and the Kushites and may have given the Thebans a middleman position in this trade. This is uncertain, however, since the Hyksos and Kushite rulers continued to maintain a defensive alliance. The aim of this alliance was to compel the Thebans to fight on two fronts, if they attacked either their northern or southern neighbour.[1]

Kamose appears to have campaigned against the Kushites prior to his final drive against the Hyksos. No doubt, his aim was to secure Aswan against Kushite attack prior to waging war in the north. During his war against the Hyksos, Kamose intercepted a letter that Aweserre was sending to the King of Kush. In this letter Aweserre complained that the new King of Kush had not observed standard protocol by informing Aweserre of his accession. This failure is probably an indication of how effective Theban policing of the desert routes had become at this time.

Plate 42

In the captured letter, Aweserre urged the King of Kush to honour his commitment to attack the Thebans; if the attack were successful, the Hyksos and Kushites could divide the Theban domain between

Fig. 35

them. By this time, however, the Kushites appear to have been unable to assist their allies. A graffito carved on a rock at Arminna East records the names of Kamose and his Viceroy ('King's Son') Teti. This inscription suggests that Kamose may have taken possession of Lower Nubia and established the New Kingdom administration of that area.[2] The Egyptian occupation evidently encountered no serious opposition. Few Kushite soldiers were stationed in Lower Nubia and the resident Egyptians and C-Group people probably switched sides with little difficulty.

THE MEDJAY IN LOWER NUBIA

The power of the New Kingdom Pharaohs was based on their control of a standing army that was larger and more specialized than the armies of the Middle Kingdom had been. During the New Kingdom, foreign recruits and prisoners of war were to play an increasingly prominent role in this army. The Pharaohs of the Seventeenth Dynasty seem to have been unable or unwilling to enlist Nubians but enrolled large numbers of Medjay recruits from the Eastern Desert, particularly as scouts and light infantry. Although little is known about the archaeology of the Eastern Desert, it is generally accepted that these Medjay were buried in the so-called 'Pan-Graves'. These graves are found throughout the southern part of Egypt, which was governed by the early rulers of the Seventeenth Dynasty. The bodies, clad in leather garments and wearing

Fig. 36

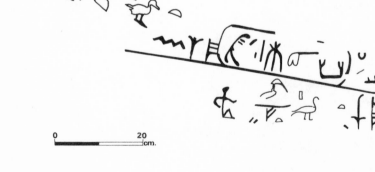

0 ⎯⎯⎯ 20 cm.

shell-plaque jewellery, were interred in circular grave pits, on their right
side facing west. The pottery found in these graves is a distinctive
manifestation of the C-Horizon. The black-topped vessels frequently
have a thickened lip that is separated from the red portion of the vessel
by an incised line. Rough brown ware vessels are either undecorated or
incised with patterns of oblique lines. The graves were covered with a
gravel mound delimited by a ring of stones or mud brick. Unplundered
graves often contain Egyptian axes and daggers, such as might be
expected to occur with professional soldiers, as well as gold and other
intrinsically valuable jewellery. Although the archaeological evidence
indicates that the descendants of these immigrants were completely
Egyptianized by the end of the Hyksos period, many probably continued
to serve in the Egyptian army and police force for the duration of the
New Kingdom.[3]

Pan-Grave interments are also found in Lower Nubia, either on the
margin of C-Group cemeteries or in small cemeteries of their own farther
back in the desert. These graves are generally dated to the Second
Intermediate Period and the New Kingdom.[4] While some may belong
to immigrants who filtered into Lower Nubia during the Second
Intermediate Period, it seems likely that most of the Medjay who settled
in Lower Nubia did so as part of the New Kingdom occupation force
or as allies whom the Egyptians allowed to settle in conquered territory.
Pan-Grave pottery has been found inside Egyptian fortresses at El-Kab
(in Upper Egypt), Quban, and Serra East and it is likely that these

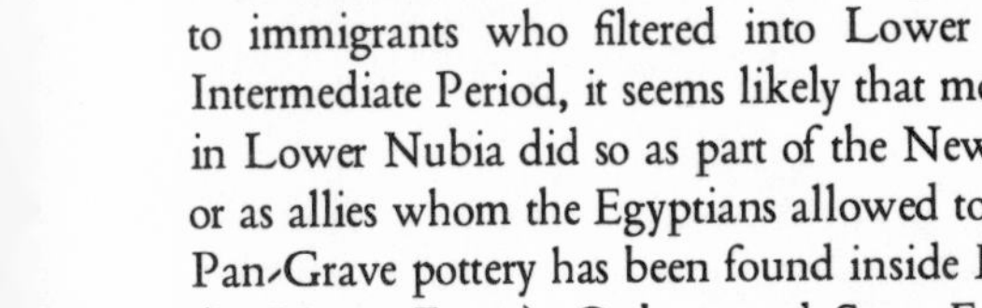

Fig. 37

Plate 43

Fig. 35 *Arminna East graffito
commemorating viceroys of Kings
Kamose and Ahmose (after
Simpson 1963 : 27)*

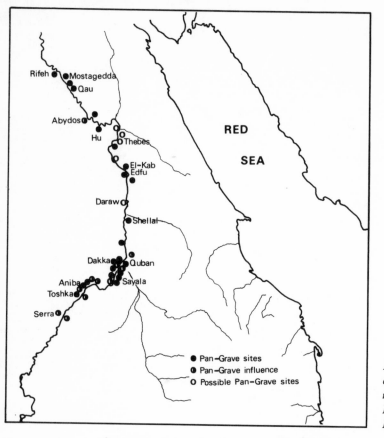

Fig. 36 Location
of Pan-Grave sites
in Egypt and
Nubia (after
Bietak 1966 : fig. 5)

forts were garrisoned at least in part by Medjay mercenaries. Pan-Grave
cemeteries generally occur in areas that were already centres of C-Group
population, suggesting that small colonies of Medjay were stationed in
these areas to keep watch over the indigenous inhabitants.[5] Especially
if the Medjay and C-Group had formerly been at odds over the use of
the east bank of the Nile, the Medjay would have been well suited to
keep watch over their rivals.

THE CONQUEST OF KUSH

Kamose was succeeded by his brother, Ahmose, whom Egyptians
later counted as being the founder of the Eighteenth Dynasty and

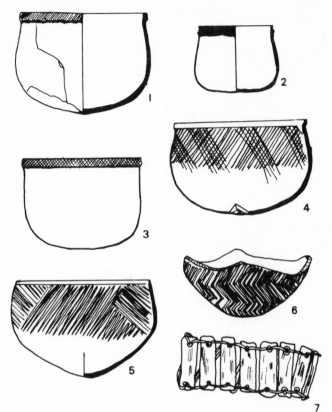

Fig. 37 Pan-Grave artefacts: 1, 2 black-topped pottery; 3–6 incised brown or grey pottery; 7 shell-plaque arm band (after Bietak 1968: pl. 16)

the first Pharaoh of the New Kingdom. Ahmose's energies were directed mainly towards crushing the power of the Hyksos in Egypt and capturing their bases in southern Palestine. It was not until his twenty-second regnal year that Ahmose is known to have directed his attention towards Nubia. In spite of this, two Egyptian officials, Djehuty and Sataiyit, were Viceroys of Nubia during his reign, while Thuwre, who was Commandant of Buhen at that time (and who held the same title as Sepedhor had in the service of the King of Kush), was to be appointed Viceroy by his successor.[6] During Ahmose's reign, a small temple was erected at Buhen, probably as part of the work of rehabilitation that the Egyptians were carrying out at this and other Middle Kingdom forts in Lower Nubia. Ahmose is reported to have slaughtered many Nubians, but it is unclear how far south his conquests carried him. It has been suggested that he built the first New Kingdom temple at Sai Island, but the inscription referring to him and his queen may date from later times. Amenhotep I, who succeeded Ahmose in 1545, boasts of having captured a Nubian chieftain in the midst of his army when he ascended the river to Kush.[7] Inscriptions of his Viceroy, dated to Amenhotep's seventh and eighth regnal years, have been found at Semna and Uronarti.[8]

In spite of Egyptian advances, the Kushite heartland seems to have remained intact until the second regnal year of Amenhotep's son and successor, Thutmose I. That year, an Egyptian fleet made its way through the Batn el-Hagar and established a fort at Tombos, at the northern end of the Dongola Reach. From there, the Egyptians were able to strike at Kerma, where Hintze believes Thutmose I pillaged and burned the Western Deffufa.[9] After this, Thutmose I appears to have made his way past the Fourth Cataract as far as Kurgus, where a boundary inscription carved on a rock may record his farthest penetration up-river.[10] Kurgus is located in a small gold-producing area and the hope of exploiting this gold field (later known as the gold of Karei) may have been what attracted Thutmose I into the desolate stretch of the Nile beyond the Fourth Cataract.[11] After a year of campaigning, Thutmose I

Plate 44

Fig. 38

Fig. 38 Boundary inscription of Thutmose I at Kurgus (after Arkell 1950: fig. 4)

returned to Thebes accompanied by many prisoners. The body of a ruler, probably the King of Kush, was displayed hanging head downwards from the prow of the royal ship.[12] This campaign put an end to the independent Kerma monarchy, which had played a leading role for at least several centuries of Sudanese history.

Egyptian garrisons were established at Sai, Tombos, and possibly elsewhere in Upper Nubia, no doubt to ensure that control of the sub-Saharan luxury trade would be funnelled into the hands of Egyptian officials. At this stage, however, the Egyptians appear to have been satisfied to establish indirect rule over Upper Nubia. Many local rulers were confirmed in office provided that they swore allegiance to the Pharaoh. Following the death of Thutmose I in 1505 BC, a rebellion broke out in Upper Nubia in which two sons (relatives? subjects?) of the former King of Kush played a prominent role. This uprising forced the Egyptian garrisons to retire with their cattle into the fortresses that Thutmose had built. The rebellion was firmly put down by an Egyptian army which, it was boasted, slaughtered all the Nubian men they captured except one son of the King of Kush who was brought as a prisoner to Thebes; perhaps to be trained as a puppet ruler.[13] Further uprisings had to be crushed during the co-reigns of Hatshepsut and Thutmose III and the Egyptian occupation of the Dongola Reach may have been completed at this time.[14] Hereafter, Egyptian campaigns in Nubia appear rarely to have been of importance for maintaining Egyptian hegemony in the region. More raids were directed against desert tribes than against the valley dwellers.[15]

THE ORGANIZATION AND EXPLOITATION OF NUBIA

In New Kingdom temples, the Pharaohs are frequently represented as conquerors of Nubia on one wall and of Asia on the wall opposite. This convention has led many scholars to conclude that Egypt's African and Syro-Palestinian empires were basically similar. Yet this is not the case. The rulers of the small Levantine city states were obliged to acknowledge the Pharaoh as their overlord and to pay him tribute, while Egyptian supervisors and garrisons were established in key centres to look out for the Pharaoh's interests. Yet, no attempt was made to alter the internal social or political arrangements of these states, which were based on local traditions that were as venerable as those of Egypt.

The Egyptians were well aware that in some crafts, such as weaving and metal-working, the Levantines were more skilled that they were and Asiatic deities soon found an honoured place in the Egyptian pantheon.[16]

By contrast, the Egyptians had no respect for the technology, religion, or customs of the Nubians. Like European colonists in Africa more recently, they dismissed the local technology and failed to appreciate religious practices or patterns of kinship and reciprocity that were based on principles that were radically different from their own. The Nubians were portrayed by the Egyptians as scantily clad barbarians living in thatched huts. They were also stigmatized as being feckless and indolent by the time-conscious, work-conscious administrators of the Egyptian empire. Parallels with more recent opinions of Africans occur in the punning comment that in Kush 'the monkeys (*krw*) dance and the king (*kwr*) dances' (i.e. everybody dances).[17] Given this attitude, the accomplishments of the Kerma state must have been interpreted as evidence of a barbarian menace rather than as an example of African achievement.

Plate 45

Thus while Syria and Palestine were treated as a series of subject states whose princes were to be controlled and taxed, the Nile Valley between the First and Fourth Cataracts was regarded as an area that lacked acceptable traditions of its own and therefore had to be completely reorganized along Egyptian lines. Local elites had to be either replaced by Egyptian officials or assimilated into the administrative hierarchy, while the mass of the people were destined to become peasants. The close integration of Nubia into the Egyptian system is evident in the 'tribute lists' of Thutmose III, where goods delivered to the royal treasury were recorded as taxes levied on Nubian regions and not as tribute, such as was collected from individual Syrian and Palestinian princes. This indicates that the latter were still recognized as being sovereign within their own territories while the Nubian rulers were not.[18]

The government that the Egyptians established for Nubia was largely a copy of that of Egypt. At its head was a viceroy, who at first bore the title 'King's Son and Overseer of the Southern Countries'. This was not a hereditary office and there is no evidence that the holder was a close relative of the king. He was directly responsible to the king for the administration of Nubia and sometimes brought the annual taxes of the region to Thebes to deliver them in person to the royal treasury. In the reign of Thutmose IV, this official's title was changed to 'King's Son of Kush', probably to differentiate the Viceroy Amenhotep from the heir to the throne, Amenhotep III. By the middle of the Eighteenth Dynasty, the Viceroy's jurisdiction had been extended as far north as El-Kab, thus bringing the three southern provinces of Egypt, as well as Nubia, under his sway.

Like Egypt, Nubia was divided into a northern and southern region. Each region was under the control of an *idnw* or deputy governor, whose office corresponded with that of a vizier in Egypt. The northern province was called Wawat and embraced Lower Nubia, probably as far south as Semna. Its administrative centre was at Miam (Aniba). The southern province was called Kush and its deputy governed from Amara West, at least during the Nineteenth Dynasty. As in Egypt, each major settlement had its own mayor (*haty⸳*). The armed forces, including the commanders and garrisons of fortresses, were under the control of the 'Battalion Commander of Kush'. Later in the New Kingdom, in-scriptions record the names of Chief Treasurers, Overseers of Cattle, Overseers of Granaries, Chief Priests of All the Gods; of various scribes, accountants, and attendants attached to the courts of the Viceroy and his deputies; and of the craft specialists who served under these officials.[19]

Fig. 39

The conquest of Nubia allowed the Egyptians to collect as taxes many products that they formerly had to purchase. This eliminated the Nubian middlemen and correspondingly increased the profits that accrued to the Pharaohs, who sold a portion of their Nubian tribute to neighbouring rulers. The principal materials imported from Nubia continued to be gold, ivory, ebony, and other fine woods. The Egyptians also collected considerable quantities of ostrich feathers and eggs, leopard skins, oils and gum resins (to make incense and perfumes), copper, amethyst, carnelian, feldspar, amazonite, and hematite, and selected cattle, dogs, live leopards, giraffes, and baboons. By late in the Eighteenth Dynasty, goods manufactured from wood, leather, and less often metal were being sent to Egypt. These included stools, beds, tables, armchairs, shields, bows and arrows, metal vases, and possibly sandals and boats. While Nubians may have played some role in manu-facturing these goods, they are wholly Egyptian in design and probably

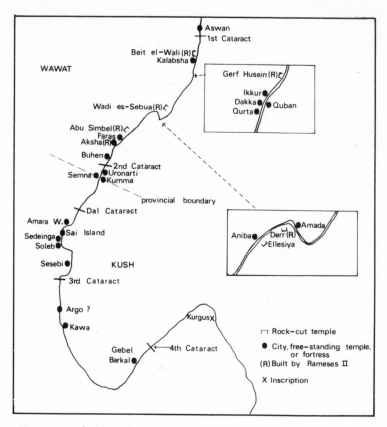

Fig. 39 Map of Nubia in the New Kingdom

the work of Egyptian craftsmen living in Nubia. In addition, a limited quantity of grain was listed among the taxes from Wawat and Kush.[20]

The Egyptians also continued to carry off Nubians and neighbouring Sudanese peoples as slaves. Some were prisoners taken in the suppression of local rebellions or in expeditions designed to ward off desert nomads. A campaign in the eighth regnal year of Thutmose IV was seemingly directed against nomads who were hindering the exploitation of the goldfields east of Wawat, while Amenhotep III carried off 740 prisoners from the wadis of Ibhet, southeast of the Second Cataract.[21] In Upper Nubia, Irm (probably Kerma) appears to have been a continuing hotbed of rebellion. Seti I records a campaign against this district, in the

Plate 46

course of which 7,000 prisoners seem to have been taken.[22] A letter of the Ramesside period contains an explicit order to send to Egypt slaves from Irm and a neighbouring region, while Ramesses III followed earlier precedents by settling many Nubians, including Irm people, as servants in the community attached to his funerary temple at Deir el-Medina.[23] Thutmose III's 'tribute lists' indicate that in his reign up to 154 Nubian slaves were being paid as taxes to the Egyptians each year. Most of these slaves came from Kush rather than Wawat.[24] They appear to have been used in Egypt mainly as militia and domestic servants.

Plate 47

Egypt's relations with the eastern Mediterranean were more complex and intimate in the New Kingdom than at any previous period. Throughout the New Kingdom, Egypt was renowned for its vast supplies of gold, control of which increased the Pharaoh's international prestige. Within Egypt itself, gold was prized more than ever before and the distribution of gold collars to the king's favoured retainers also enhanced royal power. In New Kingdom times, most of Egypt's gold came from Nubia; therefore, even if the desire to exploit the region's gold mines had not inspired the original conquest of Nubia, it must soon have become the king's principal motive for seeking to retain control of this area. Great pains were taken to expand gold production and late in the reign of Thutmose III Wawat and Kush together produced about 260 kilogrammes annually. The large amount of gold recorded in Thutmose III's 'tribute lists' contrasts strikingly with the small quantities noted for other items.[25]

Most of the gold came from mines in the upper parts of the Wadi el-Allaqi system, which in Nineteenth Dynasty inscriptions was called the region of Akita. This region was exploited far more intensively in New than in Middle Kingdom times and such mining involved arduous labour. Veins of quartz had to be broken by fire and slowly ground to powder before the gold could be extracted. The hardships of mining were compounded by the long and dangerous routes over which donkey caravans had to fetch food and drinking water from the Nile. It is therefore not surprising that most of the gruelling tasks were performed by slaves, prisoners of war, and convicts. Indeed, an Egyptian legal oath ran 'If I lie, may my nose and ears be cut off and I be sent to Kush'. Fortunately, it was only necessary to work these mines intermittently in order to produce the required amounts of gold. Traces of huts, washing tables, and smelters occur at only a few sites. The final processing of the gold was probably carried out in the fort at Quban, which had been restored after its abandonment by the Egyptians during the Second Intermediate Period.[26]

Upper Nubia produced only about one-twentieth as much gold as Wawat. Most of this gold was panned along the Nile between the Second and Third Cataracts; however, at Duweishat, a few miles up-river from Semna, many galleries and prospecting holes have been found, indicating a type of mining similar to that practised in the Eastern Desert. Duweishat's proximity to the river must have made it a relatively safe and pleasant locality to exploit. Rude stone huts are scattered about the site, but it too appears to have been worked only intermittently.[27]

A growing need for gold, as well as the depletion of the richer and more accessible deposits in the course of the Eighteenth Dynasty, seem gradually to have compelled the Egyptians to exploit poorer and more distant mines. This resulted in increasing costs and loss of life, which Seti I attempted to reduce by digging a well 120 cubits deep along the road leading to the mines. Early in the reign of Ramesses II water was located 12 cubits below the depth reached by Seti I.[28] The apparent remains of this well were located by Russian archaeologists about 55 kilometres up the Wadi el-Allaqi from its junction with the Nile.[29]

THE EGYPTIANIZATION OF NUBIA

The Pharaohs of the New Kingdom remembered the threat that a Nubian state had posed to a divided Egypt and were well aware that control of the region's wealth bolstered their own power. They were therefore anxious not simply to hold Nubia by force but to unite it indissolubly with the Egyptian state. This led them to establish Egyptian settlers and institutions in key places throughout Nubia and to attempt the Egyptianization of Nubian society. Chiefs suspected of disloyalty were replaced and if their districts were too large they were divided among a number of new appointees; however, even the descendants of the King of Kush appear to have held office as Princes of Irm as late as the reign of Thutmose III.[30] The Egyptians sought to win the loyalty of such rulers by permitting them to retain nominal sovereignty and encouraging them to live as members of the Egyptian nobility. Their sons were often taken as hostages to the Egyptian court where they were educated alongside the sons of Asiatic rulers. In the 'tribute lists' four sons of the Ruler of Irm are recorded as sent to Egypt in Thutmose III's thirty-fourth regnal year. These youths 'heard the speech of the Egyptians in the retinue of the king', which caused them to forget their own language.[31] This policy, which was also practised by recent colonial governments, produced a Nubian nobility whose cultural ties and personal friendships with the Egyptian elite were probably stronger than those with their own people. Chiefs of Lower Nubia proudly boasted titles such as 'child of the royal nursery', 'bearer of the king's folding chair' and 'king's sandal' (perhaps 'sandal maker').[32] As early as the reign of Queen Hatshepsut, the Prince of Tehkhet (Serra) used his Egyptian name Djehutyhotep in preference to his native name Pa-itsj and in his district constructed a rock-cut tomb in a wholly Egyptian style. The paintings that decorate this tomb show the prince inspecting his plantation, hunting from a chariot in the desert, and enjoying a pleasant banquet; in short, living in the same manner as an upper class Egyptian.[33] His brother and successor, Amenemhet, built an equally Egyptian-looking tomb. Although Amenemhet died

Fig. 40

Fig. 40 Plantation scene from tomb of Nubian prince, Djehutyhotep, at Debeira, Lower Nubia (after Säve-Söderbergh 1960: fig. 10)

Plates 48, 49, 50

without an heir and no later tombs are attributed to the Princes of Tehkhet, an inscription attests the survival of this office into the reign of Ramesses II.[34] Late in the Eighteenth Dynasty, Hekanefer, Prince of Miam, excavated his tomb alongside several uninscribed but similar ones in a sandstone outcrop behind the large C-Group cemetery (No. 207) at Toshka East. This seems to be a smaller and simpler version of the Theban tomb of Huy, the contemporary Viceroy of Kush.[35]

Plate 51, 52;
Fig. 41

Most of the Nubian tribute-bearers portrayed in the tomb of the vizier Rekhmire, which was decorated in the reign of Thutmose III, are shown wearing skin loincloths. A century later, the tribute presenta-tion scene in the tomb of Huy includes more than forty members of the Nubian nobility. They wear fashionable upper class Egyptian clothing

Plate 53

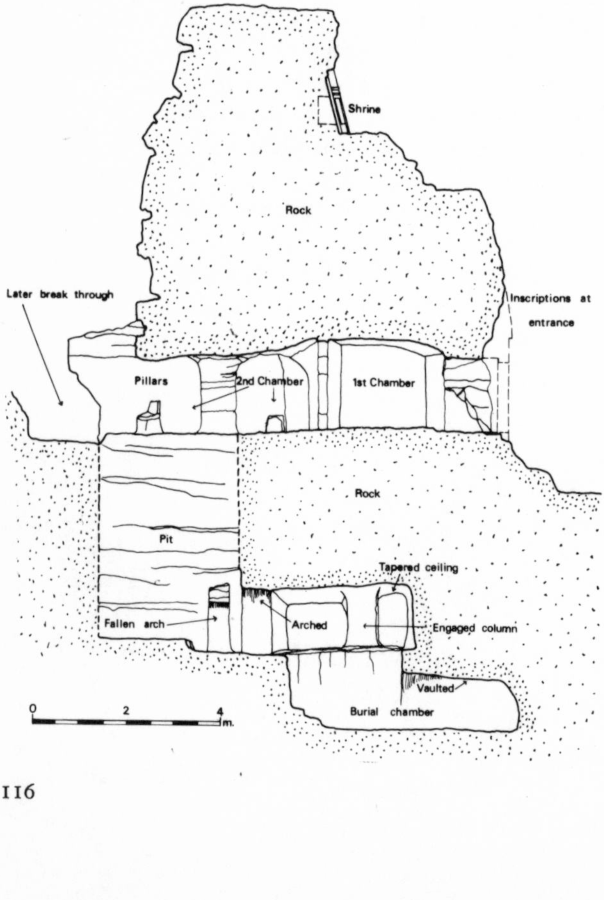

Fig. 41 Section of tomb of Hekanefer at Toshka East (after Simpson 1963a: fig. 3)

and (apart from their physical appearance) are recognizable as foreigners only by vestigal ethnic trappings, such as feather headdresses and fancy sashes. One of the women is shown riding in an Egyptian chariot pulled by two small oxen.[36] In the larger centres in Nubia it soon becomes impossible to distinguish acculturated Nubians from Egyptian immi-grants and many government officials known only by their Egyptian names may have been of Nubian descent.[37] Although archaeologists have not yet identified the residence of any Nubian princes of the late Eighteenth Dynasty, their houses were probably built along the lines of those belonging to wealthy Egyptians. Early in the reign of Amenhotep III, the Egyptians were sure enough of the loyalty of the Lower Nubians that a contingent of warriors was recruited between Quban and Aniba to wage war against the tribes of the Eastern Desert (possibly another instance of playing Nubians and Medjay against one another).[38]

It cannot be proved that all of these Egyptianized princes of Lower Nubia were necessarily descendants of C-Group headmen. Near the tomb of Hekanefer, on the side of the sandstone hills known as Gebel Agg, is a rock shrine principally adorned by a well-carved scene that dates from the New Kingdom. This scene depicts five worshippers adoring the gods Horus, Lord of Miam, Reshep (a Syrian deity), and Senwosret III. Humay, who commissioned the relief, bears the title 'Medjay of His Majesty'. He is shown holding a gazelle in one hand and a bow and arrows in the other. His brother Seninefer, who was 'Herdsman of the Cattle of Horus, Lord of Miam', bears a pair of sandals, perhaps one of the exports of the district. Below the ledge shrine was a thick deposit of pottery, apparently refuse from offerings. The pottery included many Pan-Grave sherds, which suggests that the shrine was frequented by a Pan-Grave garrison stationed nearby.[39] It is therefore possible that the Prince of Miam was a Medjay leader whom the Egyptians had made a local prince. It is possible that other princes were descended from Kushite officials who had wielded influence in parts of Lower Nubia prior to the Egyptian conquest.

A more pervasive means by which the Pharaohs sought to consolidate their hold over Nubia and its gold fields was by establishing numerous settlements throughout the region to be inhabited by Egyptians and Egyptianized Nubians. The cost of these settlements indicates the importance that the Egyptian government attached to retaining control

Plates 54, 55

of Nubia and preventing the resurgence of native polities. While practical economic, political, and military objectives determined the location of these settlements, the Egyptians attached no less importance to the religious aspect of their colonization. By making an Egyptian cult the core of each of their settlements the Egyptians saw themselves incorporating Nubia spiritually as well as culturally within the Egyptian realm. The presence of their gods gave the Egyptians a greater sense of security in their possession of the land and was meant to awe the Nubians. All of the Egyptian temples received produce from their nearby estates and some were authorized to levy duties on goods produced in their vicinity or passing them on the river.[40] These profits were used to support not only priests, administrators, and their servants, but also specialists such as traders, miners, shipbuilders, and a wide range of other craftsmen.

Some of the temples of Nubia were dedicated to Khnum, Satis, and Anukis, deities whose original cult centres were at Aswan, and to Dedun, a god who from ancient times had Nubian associations. Re-Horakhte, Ptah, and Amon, the patron deities of the three principal Egyptian religious centres, were also worshipped in many temples throughout Nubia. Distinctive Horus deities were provided for each of the major districts of Lower Nubia: Baki (Quban), Miam, and Buhen. A fourth Horus of Maha was worshipped in the vicinity of the holy mountain at Abu Simbel, while a Hathor of Ibshek was wor-shipped at Abu Simbel and Faras. By the reign of Thutmose III, the long dead Pharaoh Senwosret III was also reverenced throughout Nubia, no doubt because of his role in establishing Egyptian control over Lower Nubia in the Middle Kingdom. His chief cult centres were within the forts at Semna and Uronarti, where his boundary inscriptions had been erected. Thutmose III was also worshipped as a god in the Serra region, while Amenhotep III erected temples in Nubia where he, as well as his wife, Queen Tiy, were worshipped in their human aspect. Ramesses II was the chief deity at Aksha and was worshipped with the major state gods at Wadi es-Sebua, Gerf Husein, and Abu Simbel. In all of these temples he is represented as revering his living form, as manifested on earth or in Nubia. While the worship of reigning monarchs may have been carried to further extremes architecturally in Nubia than it was in Egypt, it is wrong to view these cults as being surreptitiously or experi-

Plate 56

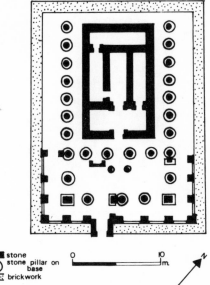

Fig. 42 New Kingdom temple at Buhen (after Emery 1965: fig. 137)

stone
stone pillar on base
brickwork

0   10
                     m.

mentally introduced among the credulous barbarians of Egypt's Nubian empire. Statues of Amenhotep III and Ramesses II were objects of worship in Egypt no less than in Nubia.[41]

The temples of the early Eighteenth Dynasty were small stone buildings consisting of a sanctuary, side rooms, and vestibule; and sometimes elaborated with colonnades, an open courtyard, and a modest entrance gate. In spite of their small size, they often were decorated with bas-reliefs of high quality.[42] The first temples seem to have been built within the major Middle Kingdom fortresses that the Egyptians renovated and continued to occupy throughout the period of the New Kingdom. Serra East and Ikkur were re-occupied along with the other forts, but the former appears to have been abandoned once the initial consolidation of Egyptian power in the region had been accomplished, while Ikkur declined in favour of an open town that grew up on the nearby plain of Dakka. Elephantine and Biggeh likewise declined in importance as the frontier vanished and they again became nothing more than Cataract trans-shipment points.[43] By contrast, Quban continued to flourish as a centre for mining activities in Lower Nubia until late in the New

Fig. 42

119

Kingdom. The fort apparently served as a state treasury while an open town grew up around it. Kor was also re-occupied.

At Aniba and Buhen, large towns grew up around the renovated fortresses, the latter's ditches being filled in to facilitate this development. At first, these expanded settlements were enclosed by a second ring of fortifications, although the new perimeter walls were of lighter construction than those around the Middle Kingdom forts. At Buhen and Aniba substantial private and public buildings were later dispersed beyond these fortifications; such as the so-called 'farmstead' or government storehouse at Aniba. The elite of these settlements were buried in the desert behind the towns. There, rock-cut tombs were adorned with small mud brick pyramids identical to those found in major New Kingdom necropoli throughout Egypt.[44] At Faras, no evidence of New Kingdom settlement was found in the area later covered by the Christian citadel; inscribed stone blocks bearing the names of Thutmose III and Ramesses II were apparently brought there from Buhen in post-Pharaonic times. Nevertheless, a small temple attributed to Queen Hatshepsut was partly cut into a rock outcrop south of the Christian citadel, while a temple of Tutankhamen together with its attendant community was located to the north of it. The latter temple foundation was called 'The Conciliation of the Gods', possibly a reference to the young king Tutankhamen's return to traditional religious usage after the Akhenaton 'heresy'.[45] The central religious complex at Faras was ringed by villages whose inhabitants cultivated nearby areas of fertile soil.

Fig. 43

Fig. 44

Fig. 45

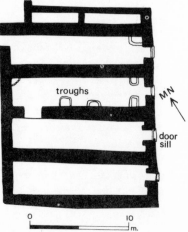

troughs

MN

door sill

Fig. 43 New Kingdom 'farmstead' or official storehouse on plain at Aniba (after Steindorff 1937)

0   10
m.

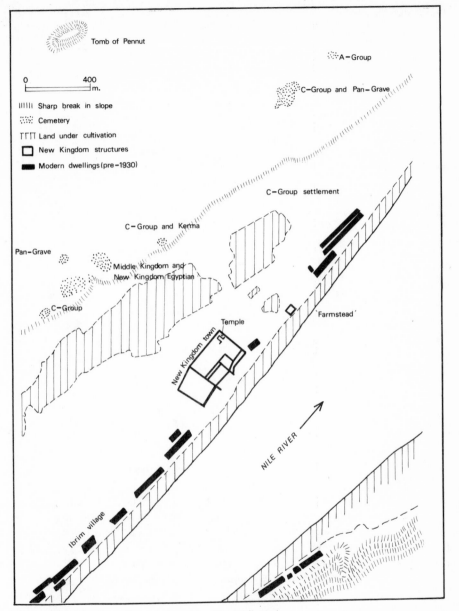

Fig. 44 Plan of Aniba in Pharaonic times (after Steindorff 1935)

Tomb of Pennut

A–Group

0   400
⊢—————⊣ m.

C–Group and Pan–Grave

|IIIII Sharp break in slope

Cemetery

ⲒⲤⲒⲤ Land under cultivation

☐ New Kingdom structures

■■ Modern dwellings (pre–1930)

C–Group settlement

C–Group and Kerma

Pan–Grave

Middle Kingdom and
New Kingdom Egyptian

C–Group

Temple

Farmstead

New Kingdom town

NILE RIVER

Ibrim village

121

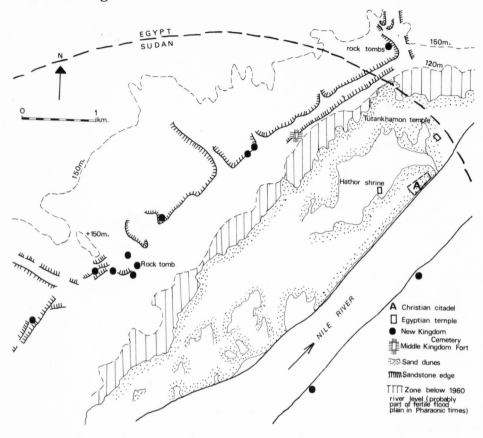

Fig. 45 Plan of Faras West in the Pharaonic period (Nordström 1961 : fig. 1)

Not long after the reconquest of Lower Nubia, the walls surrounding the Egyptian settlements no longer served for defence against attack but to control access to these settlements and for internal security. These are the same reasons that prompted the building of enclosure walls around major buildings and building complexes north of Aswan. The loose distribution of administrative buildings, temples, elite dwellings, and farming villages that eventually characterized the main towns in Lower Nubia replicates, on a reduced scale, the layout of the Theban capital and other major Egyptian centres. It therefore appears likely that these Nubian towns closely resembled provincial centres within Egypt.[46]

After the Egyptians conquered Upper Nubia, the forts in the Second Cataract region lost their strategic importance. They appear to have been used mainly for assisting transportation up and down this difficult stretch of the Nile River. Shelfak and Mirgissa were soon abandoned, the latter about the reign of Thutmose III.[47] Uronarti and Kumma were each provided with small new temples but may have been inhabited only by small colonies of priests and their servants. Only Semna is known to have retained a large garrison. A small temple was erected there in the reign of Thutmose III.[48]

Plate 57

In addition to the temples built in and around the fortress towns of Lower Nubia, others were erected in various fertile areas throughout the region. There is no evidence of substantial Egyptian settlement near these temples, which were probably intended to establish Egyptian cults among the indigenous population. No doubt the religious rites were performed by a handful of resident Egyptian priests, at least during the early years of Egyptian rule. The temples that were erected in the Eighteenth Dynasty were small and lacked strong enclosure walls; suggesting that the Egyptians soon regarded all parts of Lower Nubia as fully pacified. Between the reigns of Thutmose I and Thutmose III, free-standing temples apparently were constructed at Kalabsha, Dakka, and Qurta, while at Amada a particularly fine temple was finished by Amenhotep II, and another was built at Wadi es-Sebua by Amenhotep III.[49] Temples with their sanctuaries and sometimes other chambers carved out of rock cliffs flanking the Nile were constructed by Hatshepsut at Faras, by Thutmose III at Ellesiya, and by Horemheb at Abu Hoda. The latter king also constructed a rock-cut temple at Gebel es-Silsila just north of Aswan, where he is represented returning in triumph with Nubian prisoners. These structures presaged the larger rock-cut temples that were to be built in Lower Nubia later in the New Kingdom.[50] Shrines and stelae were also cut in the very high and conspicuous cliffs at Qasr Ibrim and Gebel Adda beginning early in the New Kingdom.[51] There may also have been a New Kingdom temple atop that headland at Qasr Ibrim.

Plate 58

Plate 59

In the course of his long reign, Ramesses II (1290–1224 BC) constructed a number of temples throughout Lower Nubia that were

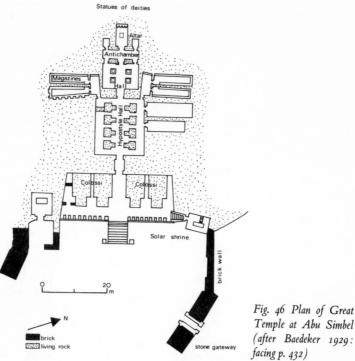

Fig. 46 Plan of Great
Temple at Abu Simbel
(after Baedeker 1929:
facing p. 432)

Plate 60;
Fig. 46

Plate 61

wholly or partially cut from the solid rock. The largest and finest of these
is the Great Temple hewn in the cliffs on the west bank of the Nile at
Abu Simbel. This temple was finished early in the reign of Ramesses II
and may have been begun by his father, Seti I. The pylon of the temple
is adorned with four seated statues of the king each over 19.5 metres
high. Behind this façade, a series of halls penetrates 55 metres into the
rock to a small sanctuary containing large seated statues of the imperial
gods Ptah, Amon, and Re-Horakhte, and of Ramesses II. Flanking
these axial chambers are six rock-cut storerooms and two sacristies.
The temple was decorated with painted bas-reliefs depicting religious
ceremonies and Ramesses II's military exploits in Syria and the Sudan.
The orientation of the temple permitted the light of the rising sun to
penetrate the sanctuary at certain times of the year.[52]

Just north of the Great Temple, Ramesses II ordered a smaller rock-cut temple for the worship of the goddess Hathor and apparently also of his principal wife, Nefertari. The façade of this temple is 28 metres long and 12 metres high and is decorated with six statues of the royal couple who stand wearing elaborate crowns. Both of these temples were probably endowed with estates at Farek, opposite Abu Simbel, and elsewhere. Farther north, Ramesses II constructed temples partially cut in the rock at Derr, Wadi es-Sebua, Gerf Husein, and Beit el-Wali. Wadi es-Sebua is the closest to being a conventional free-standing New Kingdom temple, but is much larger than any of the Eighteenth Dynasty temples in Lower Nubia. The temple of Ptah at Gerf Husein was built under the administration of Setaw, the last of Ramesses II's Viceroys. Although modelled on the Great Temple at Abu Simbel, this one, like many of Ramesses II's later works, is poorly constructed and its decoration is generally shoddy and debased. South of Abu Simbel, the banks of the river are flat; therefore at Aksha, Ramesses II erected a free-standing temple along the same lines as those he erected in Egypt and Upper Nubia.[53]

Plates 62, 63

Plate 64

Ramesses II and probably other Pharaohs used prisoners of war to carry out their building operations in Lower Nubia. An inscription records that Ramesses II used 'multitudes of workmen from the captivity of his sword in every land' for building operations at Abu Simbel,[54] while another inscription states that in his forty-fourth regnal year Libyan captives helped to build the temple at Wadi es-Sebua.[55] Various kings also endowed the temples of Nubia with foreign slaves; for example, Ramesses I donated captives to the temple at Buhen.[56] Many may have been skilled craftsmen rather than manual labourers. The Libyan and Asiatic prisoners who were sent to Nubia either on short tours of duty to perform specific projects or as chattel to be settled on temple estates must have added a cosmopolitan flavour to an already ethnically diverse population.

Much less is known about Egyptian colonization in Upper Nubia. The most obvious remains in that area are a number of Egyptian temples built of stone. These temples, together with rows of storerooms and associated domestic and administrative buildings, were surrounded by strong rectangular enclosure walls; all the additional construction being of mud brick. The enclosure walls had stone-lined gateways, as well as square towers at each corner and at intervals along the sides. In these respects, the temples of Upper Nubia precisely follow Egyptian models.

In some cases, however, the enclosure walls were much larger and embraced not only the temple and its service buildings but whole towns with narrow streets laid out on a grid pattern. The inclusion of so many houses within the walls of these temple communities suggests that the Egyptians who settled in Upper Nubia felt a need for more security than they did in their homeland. The temple towns appear to have served the same function as the renovated and expanded fortress towns had originally been intended to serve farther north. While the need for security appears to have been felt until later in the former Kushite heartland than it was in Lower Nubia, it is significant that extra-mural settlements eventually grew up around Amara West and nearby communities just as they did around the fortress towns of Lower Nubia. Both types of settlement were probably regarded by the Egyptians as variants of the temple-centred towns that Kemp has referred to as the 'backbone of urbanism' in New Kingdom Egypt.[57]

Most of the Egyptian foundations known in Upper Nubia date from the late Eighteenth and Nineteenth Dynasties and have been found between the Dal and the Third Cataracts. The northernmost of these sites is the walled town of Amara West (then probably an island). It may have been founded in the Eighteenth Dynasty but the surviving ruins are mainly the work of Seti I and Ramesses II. This town was occupied continuously until the end of the New Kingdom and appears to have been the residence of the Deputy of Kush and there-fore the chief administrative centre for Upper Nubia.[58] There was a similar walled town on the northeast shore of Sai Island which con-tained several stone temples, some dating as early as the reign of Amen-hotep II. Sai Island was probably occupied by the Egyptians from the conquest of Upper Nubia to the end of the New Kingdom.[59] A short distance up-river were the large temples at Soleb and Sedeinga, which were built by Amenhotep III for the worship of himself and his consort Queen Tiy. Soleb is generally considered to be the finest Egyptian temple in Nubia and resembles in many details one built at Luxor (in the Theban capital) earlier in the reign of Amenhotep III. Soleb underwent a number of enlargements and alterations during its founder's

Plate 65

Plate 66
Fig. 47

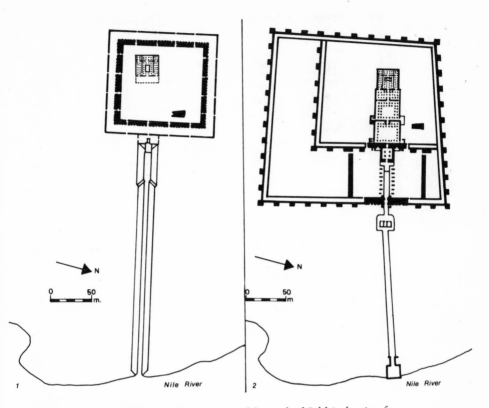

Fig. 47 Earliest and final phases in the construction of the temple of Soleb in the reign of Amenhotep III. In the first phase the temple is connected to the river by a small canal (Giorgini 1962: figs 1 and 3)

reign and was adorned with many artistic masterpieces including granite lions and rams that were removed to Gebel Barkal by Nubian rulers centuries later. The graves at Soleb do not suggest that the priestly colony remained there past the end of the Eighteenth Dynasty.[60] At Sesebi three temples were erected on a single platform early in the reign of Amenhotep's successor Akhenaton. These formed the nucleus of a walled town 270 metres long and 200 metres wide.[61] The ditched but apparently unwalled enclosures under the major constructions both at Sesebi and Soleb may date from early in the Eighteenth Dynasty, or be associated with the later building operations that went on at these sites.

Plate 67

Fig. 48

127

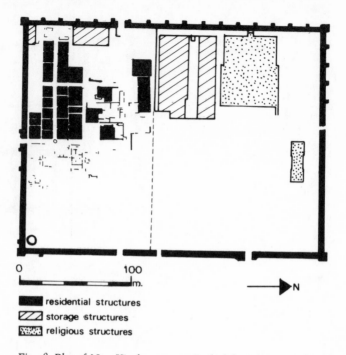

0   100
m.

➤N

■ residential structures
▨ storage structures
▦ religious structures

Fig. 48 Plan of New Kingdom town at Sesebi (after Fairman 1938, as simplified in Kemp 1972: fig. 1)

None of the sites mentioned so far occurs in a region of exceptional agricultural prosperity, even by Nubian standards. This suggests that they may have been largely concerned with the management of gold panning or other specialized operations in this region.

Only two Egyptian colonies are known for certain in the Dongola Reach, although the region has much arable land and was probably the most populous section of Nubia during the New Kingdom. Nothing that dates from the New Kingdom has been found at Kerma, which suggests that the site may have been ignored deliberately because of its former political connotations. In its place, the Egyptians may have favoured the little explored site of Tabo, on the nearby Island of Argo; although it is also possible that the stone blocks from New Kingdom temples that were found there may have been transported to the site at a later date.[62] Kawa, which is only a short distance south of Argo, is believed to be the site of Akhenaton's town of Gem/aton, although the earliest dated structure there is a small temple built by Tutankhamen and usurped by Ramesses II.[63] Inscriptions from Gebel Barkal (Napata) suggest that this important settlement at the southern end of the Dongola Reach was already in existence in the reign of Thutmose II. Yet in later times it was Thutmose III who was regarded as the founder of the Amon cult there.[64] Thutmose III's successor, Amenhotep II, records that he sacrificed seven captive princes on his return from a successful campaign in southwestern Asia and had the body of one of these victims hung on the walls of Napata;[65] no doubt to display the power of the king on the southern frontiers of his dominion. His successor, Thutmose IV, also left monuments at Gebel Barkal. While at least two finely decorated temples were built there in the Eighteenth Dynasty, the great Amon temple that was later to make Gebel Barkal a southern counterpart of Karnak was the work of Horemheb and the early Pharaohs of the Nineteenth Dynasty. All of these temples were erected at the foot of a prominent butte that the Egyptians called the 'Holy Mountain' and regarded as the Throne of Amon-Re, Lord of the Winds.[66] While the absence of known Egyptian sites between Kawa and Napata may indicate that these were the termini of a desert route that cut off the great bend of the Nile, future surveys may reveal the existence of more settlements in the Dongola area.

During the New Kingdom, the economy of Nubia became considerably more complex than it had been before and was remodelled along Egyptian lines. Although pastoralism and hunting remained important, especially in poorer localities,[67] a portion of the herd or catch was now likely owed to the government or to a local temple. At the same time, community or kinship based patterns of landholding were replaced by Egyptian-style estates. Most, if not all, of the Nubians must eventually have found themselves working as peasant farmers on land that was owned by the crown, local princes, government administrators, and by the temples that were built throughout the region. Certain temples in Egypt were also endowed with land and the right to exploit or tax certain resources in Nubia. An inscription found near the Third Cataract suggests that Seti I endowed his funerary temple at Abydos with land in that area and with various other privileges, including the right to wash for gold.[68]

This shift in patterns of land and resources ownership seems to have been accompanied by the development of more intensive agriculture. The plantation scene in the tomb of the Nubian prince Djehutyhotep suggests that he may have been producing dates for export to Egypt. It is also possible that the distinction between black and brown skinned workmen in this scene is between Lower Nubians who worked as serfs on his estates and negro slaves who came from farther south. Bee-keeping, fishing, and wine production are attested in the vicinity of the Third Cataract and there were probably similar specializations in Lower Nubia.[69] Basin agriculture was impossible throughout most of Nubia because of the terrain, but the shaduf (a manual water hoist) became known to the Egyptians sometime during the New Kingdom and the application of this device farther south would have increased agricultural productivity, particularly in Lower Nubia.[70] Despite these improvements grain still had to be sent from Egypt to feed and pay government employees.

In the reign of Ramesses VI, an important official recorded the dona-tion of a plot of land to support the cult of a royal statue at Aniba.[71] Two similar donations to a temple at Faras were recorded at Abu Simbel in the reign of Ramesses II,[72] while the prices quoted for the sale of land in a Ramesside inscription addressed to Horus, Lord of Buhen, seem considerably higher than the price of similar land in Egypt.[73] These high prices probably reflect the scarcity of good land in Nubia and the importance that was therefore attached to owning it.

The Egyptians imposed not only their economic system but also their concepts of class stratification upon the people of Nubia. In Nubia, however, ethnic inequalities increased the complexity of the social picture. The families of native rulers who were willing to col-laborate with the Egyptians were assimilated into the upper ranks of colonial society, although they were outnumbered and outclassed in power by Egyptian senior administrators. The majority of Nubians were probably relatively worse off than before, working as serfs on lands owned either by Egyptians or by Egyptianized Nubians who had effectively renounced all the ties of patronage and kinship that formerly linked them to their tribesmen. These Nubians were also generally outclassed by the Egyptian freemen who lived in Nubia. Slaves were protected from grim Nubian customs such as retainer sacrifice, but increased in numbers and came from more diverse ethnic origins. The lot of those who were employed in government service, and particularly in mining operations, was probably harsher than that experienced in daily life at Kerma or in traditional Nubian society generally.

THE DISAPPEARANCE OF THE C/GROUP

The population of Lower Nubia reached its highest figure prior to the Christian era early in the New Kingdom. At that time, the region probably had between 15,000 and 20,000 inhabitants. This increase, which was a continuation of trends already underway in the Second Intermediate Period, is reflected in the distribution of sites, which now occurred not only in the more fertile and habitually inhabited areas but also in poorer ones that had not previously been exploited.[74]

Despite the tide of Egyptian colonization, the C/Group culture survived past the middle of the Eighteenth Dynasty. Scarabs bearing the name of Thutmose III provide a terminus ante quem for the final occupation of the 'Nubian castle' near Amada. Native cemeteries of this period manifest even more strikingly the mixture of C/Group, Pan/Grave, and Kerma elements that began to characterize Lower Nubia late in the Second Intermediate Period, these elements now occurring either in separate graves or more commonly together in the same grave. Black/topped pottery was still manufactured, but the shapes and decoration of C/Group pottery of the New Kingdom fell far below the standards of the preceding period. Many Nubian graves of the Eighteenth Dynasty contain Egyptian trade goods and were among the richest of all C/Group burials. Distinctively Kerma burials also occurred until late in the Eighteenth Dynasty, suggesting that the Kerma culture survived in Upper Nubia at least until that time.[75]

Some C/Group graves at Debeira appear to date from the end of the Eighteenth Dynasty. These graves have the typical rectangular shafts and circular stone coverings of the C/Group, but only Egyptian pottery is associated with them. Säve/Söderbergh has interpreted them as representing a late stage in the Egyptianization of the C/Group paralleling among ordinary people what had happened to the princely families of Lower Nubia a few generations earlier.[76] A similar explana/tion would account for the Egyptian houses containing C/Group pottery that occur far from major Egyptian centres. It has been concluded

that Egyptian customs eventually gained such ascendancy in Lower
Nubia that the native population can no longer be distinguished from
their Egyptian conquerors in terms of graves, house types, or artefacts. It
has also been concluded that this assimilation was virtually complete
by the end of the Eighteenth Dynasty and accounts for the many wholly
Egyptian-style graves that occur in late C-Group cemeteries as well as
for the entire cemeteries of such graves that are found in areas remote
from known centres of Egyptian settlement.

Fig. 49

An Egyptian-style grave in Lower Nubia consists of a rectangular
pit dug in the rock or alluvium. More elaborate ones were provided
with a subterranean end chamber or lateral niche to receive the burial.
The deceased was laid on his back rather than on his side and in rich
burials the body was placed in a wooden coffin. Grave goods, consisting

Plate 68

of food dishes, toilet objects, and shawabtis (servant figurines), were
laid in a fixed order around the corpse and the grave was covered by a
rectangular mud brick superstructure. Even in relatively small and
remote settlements, these graves have yielded Egyptian weapons and
jewellery indicating considerable local prosperity.[77]

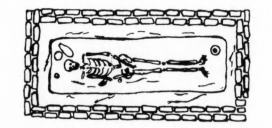

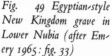

*Fig. 49 Egyptian-style
New Kingdom grave in
Lower Nubia (after Em-
ery 1965: fig. 33)*

Yet the interpretation that these are mostly the graves of acculturated Nubians is subject to serious chronological difficulties. If acculturation were taking place, the number of Egyptian graves might be expected to increase as the number of C-Group graves declined. Firth was the first to suggest that in spite of the building of new temples, Lower Nubia was in fact largely uninhabited by both Nubians and Egyptians during the later part of the New Kingdom.[78] More recently, Adams has demonstrated that, while few New Kingdom graves of either Egyptian or C-Group style can be assigned to specific reigns or even dynasties, the majority of those that can are from the first half of the Eighteenth Dynasty; with progressively fewer graves dating from the late Eighteenth and Nineteenth Dynasties and almost none later.[79] In brief, Egyptian-style graves do not become more common as C-Group ones decline in numbers as ought to be the case if acculturation were occurring. Instead, graves of both the C-Group and Egyptian traditions become less common through the Eighteenth Dynasty, although only Egyptian graves are reported for the Nineteenth Dynasty.

The simplest assumption would be that all or almost all of the Egyptian-style graves are those of Egyptian settlers. This was probably so around the fortresses and main Egyptian towns, while some Egyptian-style graves in the vicinity of outlying temples may belong to their attendant Egyptian priests. Egyptian graves associated with small out-of-the-way settlements might more speculatively be attributed to descendants of Egyptians who were already living in Nubia in the Second Intermediate Period. Yet even so one would have to assume that many Egyptians settled in Lower Nubia early in the New Kingdom, in order to account for the substantial and widely dispersed occupation attested by these graves. The theory of Egyptian origin would explain why so many Egyptian-style cemeteries are separate from C-Group ones, even when both styles of graves occur in the same locality and there are often some Egyptian-style graves in nearby and contemporary C-Group cemeteries. The latter might belong to Egyptianized Nubians, as opposed to Egyptian settlers. It would also explain Vagn Nielsen's observation that there are significant racial differences between skeletons from the two kinds of graves;[80] however, this conclusion is based on a small sample drawn from a limited area of Lower Nubia. It also conflicts with some earlier studies which suggested that there were no significant racial differences between New Kingdom and earlier population groups.[81] The strongest argument against this theory is the lack of funerary inscriptions in most cemeteries, even in association with the most prosperous graves. Had Egyptians been buried in these cemeteries at least some would have wanted to 'make their names live' with inscriptions; whereas the Nubians, unused to a tradition of literacy, may have been content without such texts.[82]

Adams has suggested that following the Egyptian conquest many Nubians were reduced to serfdom on manorial estates, while, for a time, others were allowed to maintain their tribal economies. The latter may have preserved their native culture while the new peasantry was absorbed culturally as well as economically by the Egyptian state and their graves became indistinguishable from those of Egyptian immigrants.[83] If this did happen, the prosperity of many Egyptian-style graves throughout Lower Nubia suggests that in the early stages of establishing a manorial economy the Egyptians treated the Nubians generously. At the very least, village headmen and other notables had access to luxury goods that were not within reach of the Egyptian peasantry. Routine availability of mass-produced goods from Egypt may have undercut C-Group crafts, while the propagation of Egyptian religious cults may account for the rapid and thorough adoption of Egyptian burial practices. In order to persuade the people of Lower Nubia to accept Egyptian sovereignty in toto, the Egyptian government may have been prepared to extend economic inducements to at least a part of Nubian society that were not normally extended to the peasantry of Egypt.

We can further speculate that the apparent disappearance of population during the late Eighteenth and Nineteenth Dynasties resulted from the increasingly comprehensive and exploitative nature of the Egyptian manorial economy. As the burden of taxes and debts increased, Egyptian-style graves became simpler and grave offerings were dispensed with, so that these graves can no longer be identified in the archaeological record. As Adams points out, the graves of peasants have seldom been identified for any of the great civilizations of antiquity.[84] The disappearance of the C-Group may indicate that the last remnants of tribal groupings had been absorbed into a manorial economy by the end of the Eighteenth Dynasty. Some Nubians may have avoided this by joining the Medjay of the Eastern Desert, but the control that the Egyptians exercised over all of Nubia makes it unlikely that many made their way south to Dongola.

LOWER NUBIA IN THE LATE NEW KINGDOM

Unfortunately, even this special pleading does not explain the evidence of population decline in the New Kingdom or resolve the discrepancies between archaeological and textual data. The main problem is that upper class as well as ordinary graves declined in number during the New Kingdom. In the main cemetery at Aniba, 74 graves have been accurately dated to the Eighteenth Dynasty, but only 25 to the Nine, teenth, and two to the Twentieth.[85] This makes it harder to avoid the conclusion that Ramesses II was building his temples in a land that was rapidly becoming devoid of population.

Firth and Adams have attributed this population decline to lower flood levels that narrowed the floodplain and reduced agricultural productivity below an acceptable level. Firth attributed the lower levels to erosion of the river bed; Adams to a decline in the annual volume of the Nile flood.[86] There is some evidence of reduced rainfall over East Africa after 1500 BC,[87] but the Egyptian floodplain does not appear to have been substantially lower in the New Kingdom than it was during the last century. The Eighteenth and Nineteenth Dynasties were periods of exceptional prosperity in Egypt and there is no evidence of an agricultural crisis at that time. Likewise, the significant cultural develop, ment in Upper Nubia during the first millennium BC suggests that the more sensitive Nubian floodplain was not seriously affected by lower flood levels. Ecological changes do not appear to have been of great importance even as contributing factors when it comes to accounting for the disappearance of population in Lower Nubia.

Firth also attributed a loss of population to conscription for the foreign wars of Ramesses II.[88] The population of Lower Nubia may have been depleted by conscription and mining corvees. Yet, it seems unlikely that the temple estates, which appear to have grown more numerous into the reign of Ramesses II, would have acquiesced to policies that were wholly injurious to their own economic activities. With rare exceptions, Egyptian temples were centres of complex, largely agrarian based economies whose operations depended upon

sizable dependent populations. One would assume that such populations as were drawn off were taken largely from communities that lay
outside the orbit of the larger estates.

It is possible that in the late New Kingdom the population of Lower
Nubia was largely concentrated in the vicinity of major Egyptian
settlements, near to which the agrarian estates would also have tended to
be located. New monuments were being erected at Quban as late as the
reign of Ramesses X, while a tomb belonging to the Viceroy Pinhasi at
Aniba dates from the end of the Twentieth Dynasty.[89] Earlier in that
dynasty, Pennut, who was Deputy of Wawat, 'Chief of the Quarry
Service' and 'Steward of Horus, Lord of Miam', constructed a small but
finely decorated tomb in the cliffs behind Aniba. The inscriptions in his
tomb mention the dedication of a statue of Ramesses VI in the temple of
Ramesses II at Derr (which must still have been in use at this time) and
the endowment of agricultural land for cult purposes. These inscriptions
also mention relatives who were 'Royal Treasurer in Miam' and 'Mayor
of Miam' and whose tombs have not been located.[90] This suggests
that, in spite of a dearth of archaeological evidence, the administration
of Nubia and many of its cults continued to function; which, in turn,
presupposes a local peasantry.

Cartouches of Ramesses IV have been found at Gerf Husein, Buhen,
and on stone blocks re-used in the final rebuilding of the official residence

Plate 69;
Fig. 50

Fig. 50 Plan of the tomb of Pennut at Aniba, Twentieth Dynasty (after Steindorff 1937)

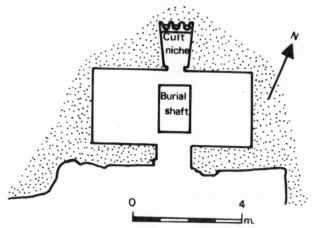

in the fort at Dorginarti. The latter inscriptions, together with some small finds, indicate that this island fortress at the foot of the Second Cataract was of some importance late in the New Kingdom. Presumably contact with Upper Nubia was still of sufficient importance for building operations to be undertaken there. One ostracon from Dorginarti records the arrival of grain, presumably to feed the local garrison.[91]

Plate 70

Soon after the end of the Twentieth Dynasty, written records as well as archaeological data concerning Lower Nubia fail completely and it must be assumed that the region once again lacked a settled population. The final abandonment is probably correlated with a sharp decline in Nubian gold production in the course of the late Nineteenth and Twentieth Dynasties. Intensive exploitation seems to have been exhaust-ing increasingly remote mines in the Wadi el-Allaqi system, while the Egyptian government was wracked by barbarian invasions on its northern frontiers and had to cope with vexatious internal problems. Thus the Egyptians were unable to invest the labour and capital necessary to maintain production even though gold was still important for purchasing the support of foreign rulers.[92] Since goldmining had been important in promoting Egyptian settlement in Lower Nubia, its cessation, as well as increasing political instability, was probably a major consideration leading to the Egyptian abandonment of the region. Government officials, native princes, and temple staffs could have moved to Egypt or in some cases settled farther south in the Sudan, taking their servants and peasant labourers with them. For 500 years Lower Nubia had been the focus of an intensive programme of Egyptianization; now, apart from a few military garrisons, it was again abandoned to the nomads of the Eastern Desert.

CHAPTER VIII

The Kingdom of Kush

UPPER NUBIA AFTER THE NEW KINGDOM

The Pharaohs of the New Kingdom made increasing use of foreigners, many of whom were taken into royal service from defeated armies. By the Twentieth Dynasty Libyans, Semites, and people of Aegean origin, as well as Nubians, held important positions at court and throughout Egypt. As royal power weakened, the many foreign troops who served in the Egyptian army began to play an important role in the internal politics of Egypt. In the reign of Ramesses III (1182–1151 BC), a captain of the Nubian archers was drawn into a conspiracy of regicide. It is unknown whether this man was of Egyptian or Nubian origin, but his military command made him important to the conspirators. The Viceroy of Kush does not appear to have been involved in this plot, since his son eventually succeeded him and held office under Ramesses IV. Although the kings now ruled from the Delta rather than from Thebes, they could still count on the loyalty of their viceroys. The names of Ramesses VI and the Viceroy Siese appear together at Amara, and Nubian taxes were paid until the reign of Ramesses XI. The one indication of slackening royal control was a tendency for the viceregal office to pass from father to son with growing frequency.[1]

It appears that by the end of the Twentieth Dynasty the king was no longer able to control his mercenaries, and Nubian and Libyan factions within the army began to compete for power.[2] In the reign of Ramesses XI, the Viceroy of Kush was Pinhasi, who may have been of Nubian origin and who, unlike his predecessors, assumed personal control of his province's armed forces.[3] Pinhasi and his troops advanced northward into central Egypt and destroyed the town of Hardai, possibly in a vain effort to check the growing power of the Libyans. By the nineteenth regnal year of Ramesses XI (1080 BC), Herihor, who appears to have been of Libyan origin and was probably a military officer, assumed de facto control of Upper Egypt. He styled himself CommanderinChief of the Egyptian army, High Priest of Amon, and Viceroy of Kush and eventually, before predeceasing Ramesses XI, he took the title of king. In the northern part of Egypt, Ramesses XI was eventually succeeded by Nesbanebded (Smendes I) who like Herihor seems to have had no natural right to the throne. Herihor's descendants were to control Upper Egypt for four generations. They retained most of his religious and military titles, although only one of them (Pinudjem I) asserted his claim to be a Pharaoh against Nesbanebded's descendants, who controlled northern Egypt from their capital at Tanis in the eastern Delta. Relations between Thebes and Tanis appear to have been generally amicable, with marital ties linking the two ruling families. Although both Herihor and his son Piankh claimed to be Viceroys of Kush, it is doubtful that either was able to exercise any of the prerogatives of the office. Piankh is known to have campaigned in the south as late as the twenty-eighth year of Ramesses XI and may have done so against Pinhasi, who is conjectured to have withdrawn to Nubia after he was defeated by the Libyans.[4] The absence of further references to the vice-royalty indicates that the Egyptians exercised little if any control over Nubia after the Twentieth Dynasty.

Unfortunately, it is not known what happened in Upper Nubia between 1070 and 850 BC. The Egyptian towns north of the Third Cataract seem to have been abandoned by the end of the New Kingdom and some Egyptologists have doubted that there were any Egyptians living in Upper Nubia after that time.[5] Others have suggested that nominal Egyptian sovereignty was upheld by the priests at Gebel Barkal, who remained in contact with the priesthood of Amon at Thebes, or by Egyptian priests, officials, and traders who had remained in Upper Nubia and intermarried with the local population to form a 'government in exile' in opposition to the Libyan rulers in Egypt.[6] Goedicke has tentatively suggested, on religious and stylistic grounds, that the cartouches of an unidentified king at Kawa and Gebel Barkal may date as early as the Twenty-first Dynasty.[7] These might indicate that at least one Egyptian or Egyptianized Nubian ruled over an independent kingdom in Upper Nubia. It has also been argued that Shoshenq I (945–924 BC) invaded Nubia in an attempt to secure goods from the south and that the Nubian troops who served in his later Palestinian campaign may have been taken prisoner by him at this time.[8] His intervention in Nubia, if it occurred, appears to have produced no lasting results.

The Kingdom of Kush

Plate 71

The important role that was played by the Amon cult at Gebel Barkal after 750 BC has been interpreted as evidence that this cult was maintained there without interruption since the end of the New Kingdom. This, in turn, suggests that many Egyptian traditions may have been preserved in Upper Nubia during the period following the Egyptian withdrawal. It is possible, however, that the Amon cult was revived about 750 BC by Nubian rulers who judged that by patronizing the principal Theban deity they would win the support of that city against the Libyan dynasts to the north. Some trade probably continued between Nubia and Egypt but it is unknown whether such contact encouraged the survival of Egyptian customs or whether Nubia as a whole returned to an essentially tribal way of life. The Dongola Reach may not have had to regress greatly if, as some believe, the Egyptianization of that region was superficial by comparison with what had taken place north of the Third Cataract.

THE NAPATAN KINGDOM

Plate 72;
Fig. 51

Fig. 52

Archaeological evidence for the history of Upper Nubia recommences c. 850 BC when the first interments appear to have been made in what was to become the royal cemetery at Kurru a few miles downstream from Gebel Barkal. There it is possible to trace the rise of a family that won control of Nubia and for a century was to rule Egypt as well. The highest ground in the cemetery is occupied by thirteen tumuli that Reisner has plausibly ordered chronologically in terms of increasing size and complexity. He estimated that these tumuli represent the first five or six generations of the dynasty, preceding a certain King Kashta, whose influence extended into Upper Egypt sometime before 750 BC. The most prominent location in the cemetery is occupied by a small tumulus (Tumulus I) covering a grave oriented north to south and with a simple burial niche on the west side. Reisner judged this to be the oldest grave in the cemetery. In later tumuli nearby, the burial pit was covered with stone slabs, while lower down the slope were two tumuli surrounded by rings of masonry and enclosed with horseshoe shaped stone walls. One of these tumuli had a mud brick chapel against its east face. Still farther down were eight burial pits covered by square sandstone mastabas equipped with masonry chapels and rectangular sandstone enclosure walls. Two of the latest mastabas, which are

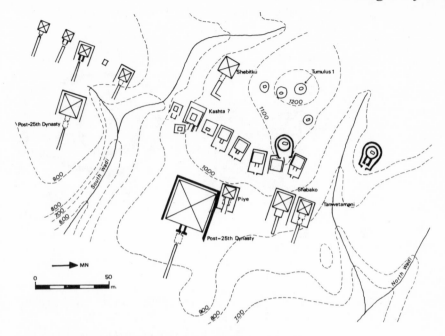

Fig. 51 Plan of the cemetery at Kurru (after Dunham 1950: map II)

attributed to the reign of Kashta, had burial pits oriented east to west in traditional Egyptian style. This was to be the orientation of all Nubian royal tombs from that time onwards.

Further advances can be observed in the reign of Kashta's successor Piye (the name was formerly read Piankhi), when corbelled vaults were used to cover the burial pits. In order that the vault of Piye's tomb could be finished prior to his funeral, a stairway was cut through the rock that opened into the east end of the burial chamber through a rock-cut doorway. The superstructure of his tomb was probably a steep-sided pyramid like those of later Nubian royal burials. Three of Piye's successors, Shabako, Shebitku, and Tanwetamani were also interred at Kurru. To avoid having to build pyramids over fill, the stairways of these later tombs were cut more deeply and the last steps ran through a rock tunnel before reaching burial chambers entirely excavated in the rock. This was to remain the standard design for royal tombs until the

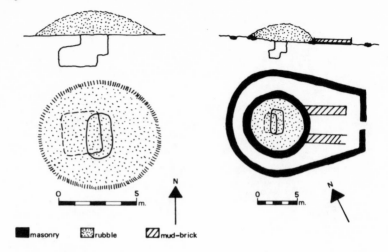

Fig. 52 Early graves at Kurru: Kurru tumuli 1 and 6 (after Dunham 1950: figs 1a; 5a)

Kushite kingdom came to an end over a millennium later, although the number of subterranean chambers varied. From Piye onwards, kings and queens were buried in separate parts of the Kurru cemetery; a custom which reflected the increasing status of these later monarchs.[9]

While the earliest graves at Kurru were humble structures architectur-ally, their contents, even after heavy plundering, indicate the prosperity of their occupants. Alongside plain stone arrowheads were found fragments of Egyptian alabaster and faience vessels as well as a con-siderable quantity of gold objects. These included necklaces, earrings, and finger rings of Egyptian workmanship. Among the beads, was a large gold nugget inscribed with hieroglyphs. Such objects suggest at least sporadic contact with Egypt. It is tempting to imagine that the men buried at Kurru were involved in trading with Egypt, which included the export of gold dust. The gold ornaments from Kurru may have been objects that the Egyptians supplied in return for raw materials.

Fig. 53

A few features of the earliest burials at Kurru are also characteristic of the Kerma culture. In both, graves were covered with a low circular mound, while the dead were laid on their side on Nubian beds. The north-south orientation of the burial chamber was also an un-Egyptian trait that occurs occasionally at Kerma. Retainer sacrifice does not appear to have been practised at Kurru, although it was practised on a substantial scale in the later phases of the civilization that the Kurru monarchy was to initiate. The stamped and incised black wares associated with this civilization also seem to be derived from the Kerma culture or the C-Horizon generally.

The growth of the new Upper Nubian state was facilitated by political concepts that appear to have been indigenous to Nubia. These included distinctly un-Egyptian practices, such as passing the throne from elder to younger brother, the confirmation of the king by the army, and a tradition of ritual regicide. There is also evidence that the native word for king *kwr* (later, in Meroitic, *qore*) was used in the Dongola area already in the New Kingdom;[10] indeed, it (or a closely cognate term) may have been used at Kerma. Calling the new kingdom Kush may have been an attempt to identify, not with the former Egyptian viceroyalty, but with the still older state of Kerma (Kush), whose memory may have been cherished in Nubian popular traditions. This does not require that a coherent tradition of government of Kerma origin had survived the Egyptian occupation of Upper Nubia. What we know about Egyptian policy in the New Kingdom makes such an eventuality unlikely. Moreover, even Egyptian customs that ought to have been familiar to the descendants of an Egyptianized elite are conspicuously lacking in the early burials in the Kurru cemetery.

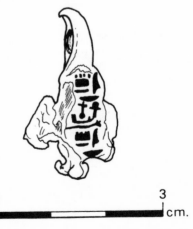

Fig. 53 Gold nugget inscribed with hieroglyphs from grave at Kurru (after Dunham 1950: fig. 2d)

0   3
cm.

There is no evidence that the rulers of Kurru were descended from the Kerma Dynasty or that their monarchy was a resurgence of the older kingdom. Kerma and Kurru were located at opposite ends of the Dongola Reach and the Kurru cemetery suggests the rapid evolution of power from humble beginnings, rather than the revival of a specific royal tradition after a long period of foreign domination. In origin, the Kushite royal house appears to have been a lineage or tribal group that possessed obvious commercial and military talents but was little affected by Egyptian customs. Such a group might have entered the region after the collapse of the New Kingdom. While there now appears to be no basis for Reisner's claim that the royal family was of Libyan origin,[11] Priese has suggested that during the New Kingdom at least some of the inhabitants of Dongola were already Nubian-speaking, while Meroitic, the official language of the later Kingdom of Kush and therefore presumably of the Kurru rulers, was originally confined to the Shendi region above the Fifth Cataract.[12] He argues that the Meroites could have occupied the Kurru region after the New Kingdom and one of their chiefs established the new Kushite Dynasty. The physical anthro-pological evidence from Kurru suggests that these rulers belonged essentially to the same stock as did the people of Kerma. The black, as opposed to brown, skinned Nubians depicted in New Kingdom art presumably lived still farther south.[13]

THE CONQUEST OF EGYPT

According to later inscriptions, the immediate predecessor of King Kashta was called Alara. He probably exercised control over most of Upper Nubia, being recognised as supreme ruler by the local dynasts of the region. His power may also have extended into the Shendi region about the Fifth Cataract, although the earliest burials identified at Meroe, which centuries later was to become the capital of the Kushite state, are from the reign of Piye.[14] Alara's brother Kashta was sufficiently in control of Nubia to be able to fish in the troubled internal affairs of Egypt. Northern Egypt was divided among a number of weak and quarrelling Libyan princes, while the Thebans periodically rebelled against Libyan rule. This dissension allowed Kashta to resume, on an enlarged scale, the struggle that had pitted Libyans against Nubians at the end of the Twentieth Dynasty. Although Kashta called himself

King of Upper and Lower Egypt, the only concrete evidence of his activities in Egypt is a stela that he erected in the temple of Khnum at Aswan. Nevertheless, Nubian garrisons were established in southern Egypt by early in the reign of Kashta's son Piye, who succeeded him *c.* 747 B C. Piye also claimed the allegiance of Libyan rulers as far north as Middle Egypt. It appears to have been he who compelled the High Priestess of Amon, who was a Libyan, to adopt his sister Amenirdis as her successor-designate.[15] At this period, the High Priestess was the kinswoman of the ruler who claimed suzerainty over Thebes and her office symbolized the alliance between the monarchy and the Amon cult. Thus, by acting as he did, Piye was reinforcing his claim to be the rightful ruler of Thebes.

In the twenty-first year of Piye's reign, a Libyan prince named Tefnakht advanced southward threatening Thebes. At the behest of his army officers who were stationed in Egypt, Piye advanced north and in a military campaign, in which he posed as the champion of Egyptian traditions against Libyan usurpers, he established his suzerainty over the whole of Egypt. This triumph, which was recorded in Egyptian hieroglyphs on a fine stela erected in the temple of Amon at Gebel Barkal, greatly enhanced the power of the Kushite kings. It also gave rise to a marked distinction between ruler and ruled that was to characterize Kushite society for many hundreds of years.[16] Piye and his successors continued to style themselves Kings of Upper and Lower Egypt and, in keeping with their new status, did many things befitting an Egyptian monarch. In Nubia, Egyptian was adopted as the written language of the state, Egyptian arts and crafts flourished, and large stone tombs and temples were erected to proclaim the power of the new rulers. Either voluntarily or by compulsion many Egyptian administrators, priests, artists, and craftsmen were brought to serve the new Pharaohs in their Upper Nubian homeland. The bodies of some of these expatri-ates may be among the mummified interments that make up a large part of the early cemetery at Sanam, an extensive settlement on the left bank of the Nile between Kurru and Gebel Barkal. The palace and storerooms at this site suggest that it, rather than Gebel Barkal, may have been the actual seat of government at this time.[17]

The adoption of Egyptian customs can best be traced in the royal cemetery at Kurru. As early as the reign of Kashta, the orientation of burials was altered to conform with Egyptian practice and in the reign of Piye the first pyramids were built. While the royal pyramids were of stone, their steep sides betray them as copies of the small mud brick pyramids of affluent Egyptians of the New Kingdom rather than of the royal pyramids of an earlier age. Within another generation, bed burials were passing out of fashion. Later, Kushite monarchs were to be mummified and provided with wooden coffins and sometimes with stone sarcophagi.

This period also saw the emergence in Upper Nubia of a government controlled economy modelled along Egyptian lines. Egyptian or Egyptian trained craftsmen turned out luxury goods for the enjoyment of the upper classes. Large amounts of standardized wheel-made pottery also occur in the major centres, suggesting that centralized control was exercised over the surpluses of many basic commodities. Although the contents of the storerooms attached to the palace at Sanam date from a later period, one room contained treasure that Piye had carried off from Egypt. Another contained elephant tusks, some possibly earmarked for Egypt.[18] Long after the Kushite kings lost control of Egypt and of the revenue that such control could provide, trading continued to supply them with Egyptian luxury goods.

The Kushite kings also strove to promote the worship of Egyptian deities throughout Nubia, particularly that of the god Amon. Piye and his successors, Shabako and Taharqa, either renovated New Kingdom temples or erected new ones at Meroe, Gebel Barkal, Sanam,

Plate 74

Kawa, and possibly Tabo, all of which appear to have flourished as administrative centres at this period. While Kawa, Gebel Barkal, and perhaps Tabo had been occupied in the New Kingdom, it remains to be determined whether any of them had been inhabited continuously

Plate 73

since that time. Taharqa, the third successor of Piye, also appears to have erected shrines at various abandoned Egyptian sites in Lower Nubia; including Semna, Buhen, and Qasr Ibrim.[19] These shrines possibly mark the location of small Nubian garrison settlements guarding the route north. In their inscriptions, the Kushite kings proclaimed their devotion to the gods of Egypt and contrasted their orthodox behaviour with the laxness of the defeated Libyans. Whatever native deities were worshipped in Nubia were no more honoured by the early Kushite kings than they had been by the Pharaohs of the New Kingdom.

Such gods were either silently syncretized with Egyptian ones or ignored altogether by these Egyptianizing monarchs.

The conquerors of Egypt were anxious to impose an Egyptian-style political organization upon their homeland and to achieve this end embraced the values and cults of the older civilization. In so doing, they were acting much as the kings and chieftains of northern Europe did when they embraced Christianity. It would be wrong to suggest that they were behaving cynically, yet it is clear that what they did rapidly consolidated the social and economic base on which their own power and that of their heirs rested. While the courtiers' graves at Sanam and Meroe reflect varying degrees of Egyptianization, the Sanam cemetery also reveals that a large un-Egyptianized element survived for several hundred years.[20] If this could happen in the shadow of the royal court, it seems likely to have been the rule in the village and tribal encampments of the Dongola and Shendi regions; the court culture of Egypt by its very nature was not something to be shared by the peasantry or labouring classes. Kushite civilization differed from that of Egypt only that in Egypt the Great Tradition had arisen out of a way of life that was largely preserved by the peasantry, whereas in Nubia it was a foreign importation that the local elite had taken upon themselves.

Yet scholars may over-estimate the Egyptianization of the Napatan elite. Politically and culturally, their monuments were concerned with validating their claim to be the rightful rulers of Egypt, while their written records were probably composed for them by Egyptians. These records may reflect an ideal better than they do reality. We have already noted peculiar institutions of Kushite kingship and indigenous titles that are only rarely or imperfectly recorded until a later age. As rulers of Kush, the Nubian kings may have behaved in a manner quite alien to their Egyptian self-image. One example of a specifically Nubian pre-occupation are the horse burials that are associated with royal interments from Piye to Tanwetamani. The rich trappings of these burials are the first evidence of a persistent Nubian infatuation with this rare and costly animal.[21]

Piye was content to be acknowledged as suzerain by the princes of Lower Egypt, who soon tried to reassert their independence. After Piye's death, his brother Shabako (716–702 BC) re-established control over the whole of Egypt. He and his successor, Shebitku, who was

Piye's son, remained securely in control of Egypt, although the expanding Assyrian empire posed a growing danger. Shebitku's younger brother, Taharqa, came to the throne *c.* 690 BC but, while he strove to consolidate his position, his armies were repeatedly defeated by the better armed and better disciplined Assyrian forces, who also enjoyed the tacit support of some Libyan princes. Thebes was occupied by an Assyrian army in 666 BC, although the Kushite Governor, Mentuemhet, continued to administer the city after the Assyrians withdrew. Taharqa's nephew Tanwetamani momentarily regained control as far north as Memphis, but his progress was halted by the return of the Assyrian king Ashurbanipal who sacked Thebes in 663 BC. By 654 BC, the Thebans acknowledged the Assyrians' puppet ruler, Psammetichus I, as their king and Nubian rule in Egypt was at an end. Lower Nubia was once again abandoned and for many years was to remain a no-man's land between Egypt and Kush.

Although they were never again to rule Egypt, the Kushite monarchy survived for over a thousand years; far longer than any one period of Egyptian unity. The prosperity of the kingdom varied through time, but throughout this period Kush was able to defend its northern border and to maintain the traditions of Pharaonic Egypt, even after these had withered away in Egypt itself.

CHAPTER IX

Conclusions

Largely because of Egypt's geography and the nature of its resources there was a tendency towards greater governmental control of the economy than in most early civilizations. Whenever Egypt had a strong central government, that government sought to extend its power south- ward along the Nile corridor in order to control trade routes, eliminate middlemen, and deal directly with the suppliers of sub-Saharan raw materials who lived in Upper Nubia. The Egyptians also exploited the raw materials of the adjacent deserts and recruited Nubian bowmen for their armies. The question arises, however, why, from the Old to the Middle to the New Kingdom, did Egyptian control penetrate farther and with greater thoroughness into Nubia? Technological advances, especially related to riverine transport, may have permitted a more effective occupation. There is, however, no direct evidence of such technological progress and it seems unlikely that the Old Kingdom society that built the Great Pyramids was unable to solve the logistical problems necessary to occupy all of Nubia.

It is also possible that the increasingly effective occupation of Nubia depended upon institutional developments, particularly in the organiza- tion of the army and the national bureaucracy. While these structures apparently grew increasingly complex, the precise significance of the changes is little understood. It seems more likely that Egypt's greater involvement in Nubia resulted from a growing need for exotic raw materials and latterly also for gold. These needs resulted both from an increasing demand for such materials by the Egyptian elite and from the Egyptian government's involvement in an expanding network of luxury trade around the eastern Mediterranean. Satisfying the demands of this network, required the increasingly efficient but also the increasingly costly exploitation of Nubia.

The effects of Egyptian policy upon the people of Lower Nubia are clear from the archaeological record. During periods of weak Egyptian government, the Lower Nubians were able to profit from trading with the Egyptians and sometimes found employment as mercenaries in the

Conclusions

Egyptian armies. During periods of strong central government, they were excluded from trading networks and Egyptian goods were difficult to obtain. The creation of a centrally managed economy early in the First Dynasty seems to have resulted in the disintegration of the A-Group culture, while during the Middle Kingdom the C-Group people were forced into local self-sufficiency.

Egyptian policy was further complicated by the impact that its economic activities had upon Upper Nubia. The centrally administered trade that Egypt carried on with the south enhanced the prestige of local chieftains who negotiated with the Egyptian traders on behalf of their own and neighbouring peoples. Such conditions favoured the development of a series of chiefdoms or rudimentary states in Upper Nubia. The earliest known was Iam, whose ruler appears to have been treated with considerable respect by Egyptian trading officials during the Sixth Dynasty. The massive border defences of the Twelfth Dynasty hint at a considerable military threat from the south, but it is only for the Kerma civilization, which reached its climax during the Second Intermediate Period, that archaeological information about a Nubian kingdom becomes available. Although the court culture of Kerma manifested strong Egyptianizing tendencies, the practice of retainer sacrifice indicates that local customs played an important role in the life of this state. While Kerma was a hierarchical society with a powerful elite and a well developed slave class, its free citizens do not appear to have been sharply divided into an elite and non-elite, as was the more evolved Egyptian society. In spite of the significant role that Kerma played in Nile Valley politics during the Second Intermediate Period, the apparent ease with which it was suppressed by the Pharaohs of the New Kingdom suggests that its military and territorial administration had not reached an advanced stage of development.

After 500 years of Egyptian rule and cultural indoctrination and another 300 years when it was apparently a political vacuum, Upper Nubia produced a powerful new kingdom which conquered and ruled Egypt for almost a century. The spectacular success of this Kushite kingdom may reflect a knowledge of statecraft derived from Kerma or other yet unknown Nubian prototypes even more so than from the years of Egyptian occupation. Some of the skills that the Kushites displayed in intervening in Egyptian politics may also have been learned from

Nubian involvement in the mercenary politics that were so important in Egypt at the end of the New Kingdom. Yet, although it ruled effectively over the middle reaches of the Nile Valley for over a millennium, the Kushite state never again challenged Egypt seriously, even during periods of weak government in the north. Much of the long term success of the early Kushite kings can perhaps be attributed to the skills with which they courted regional support in Upper Egypt and used their subsequent control of Egypt to introduce important elements of Egyptian political and economic organization into their homeland. The result was the rapid development of a class-conscious society similar in type to that of Pharaonic Egypt. The birth of the Kushite kingdom was undoubtedly the most important development in the ancient history of Nubia. The region had long been a hinterland, dominated and exploited by the Egyptians; now it witnessed the creation of a state that was able to rule Egypt for a time and, more importantly, was to be the first of a series of states that were to guarantee Nubia's sovereignty and independence. It was not until AD 1821 that Egypt was again able to control the internal affairs of the Sudan and even that control was to be swept aside after only 60 years by the Mahdist independence movement.

Notes on the Text

Full citations of references are given in alphabetical order in the bibliography.

CHAPTER I

1 Ibn Khaldun 1967.
2 Trigger 1974.
3 For the geography of the Sudanese part of Nubia, see Barbour 1961: 131–47; for Egyptian Nubia, Christophe 1963.
4 Vercoutter 1970: 166.
5 For a recent critical account of the history of Nubian archaeology, see Adams 1975.
6 Reisner 1910.
7 Firth 1912; 1915; 1927.
8 Junker 1926.
9 Emery and Kirwan 1935.
10 Lal 1967; H. Smith 1962: 64–69.
11 Emery 1963.
12 Vercoutter 1970.
13 Simpson 1963a; Säve-Söderbergh 1960; 1963a.
14 H. Smith 1966a.
15 Bietak 1968; O'Connor 1974.
16 Adams 1964: 103–9.
17 Hintze 1964.
18 Gardiner 1961: 264–66.
19 Säve-Söderbergh 1941.

CHAPTER II

1 Butzer 1971: 584.
2 De Heinzelin 1968; Butzer and Hansen 1968: 266–333.
3 Butzer and Hansen 1968: 185. De Heinzelin (1968: 50) argues that there is evidence of greater rainfall and more dispersed vegetation at this time.
4 P. Smith 1966.
5 Wendorf 1968b: 1054–57.
6 Clark 1971: 48; Churcher 1972: 126.
7 Clark 1970: 170–71.
8 Anderson 1968.
9 Wendorf 1968a: 940–46.
10 Clark 1971: 49.
11 Wendorf 1968b: 1059; Wendorf, Said and Schild 1970: 1171.
12 Wendt 1966.
13 Wendorf 1968b: 1048; cf. P. Smith 1966: 336.
14 Schild *et al* 1968.
15 Arkell 1949.
16 Clark 1973.
17 Marks 1968; Marks *et al* 1967–68: 173–74; Clark 1971: 52.
18 Butzer 1971: 587.
19 Clark 1971: 73
20 Arkell 1953.
21 Clark 1973: 63.
22 Marks 1968: 321–22; Marks *et al* 1967–68: 183–84; Wendorf 1968b: 1053–54.
23 Schild *et al* 1968.
24 Shiner 1968.
25 Marks 1968: 322; Marks *et al* 1967–68: 174–85.
26 Trigger, in press.
27 Reisner 1910: 115–27.
28 Junker 1919.
29 Shiner 1968: 626.
30 Edwards 1971: 50.
31 Nordström 1972: 17–32.

Notes on the Text

32 Nordström 1972: 28–29; Trigger 1965: 68–79.
33 Nordström 1972: 29.
34 Carlson and Sigstad 1967–68: 56.
35 Nordström 1972: 24.
36 H. Smith 1962: 64–69.
37 Nordström 1972: 27.
38 Bietak and Engelmayer 1963.
39 Adams 1975.
40 Nordström 1972: 26.
41 Nordström 1972: 21, 28.
42 Säve-Söderbergh 1941: 6.

CHAPTER III

1 Kaiser 1964.
2 Emery 1961: 139.
3 Säve-Söderbergh 1941: 7.
4 Säve-Söderbergh 1941: 6–7.
5 Helck 1970.
6 Lal 1967.
7 Kantor 1944.
8 Firth 1927: 204–12.
9 Cf. Nordström 1972: 26–27.
10 G. Björkman and T. Säve-Söderbergh, 'Seals and Seal Impressions', in Nordström 1972: 117–18.
11 H. Smith 1966a.
12 Bell 1970.
13 Nordström 1972: 31–32.
14 Note, e.g., the large 'royal' tombs erected at Naqada into the early First Dynasty: Kemp 1967: 24–25; 1973: 43.
15 E.g., Simpson 1963a: 48–49.
16 Säve-Söderbergh 1941: 7.
17 Emery 1963: 120 and personal communications from David O'Connor and P. L. Shinnie.
18 Emery 1963: 120.
19 Adams 1975.
20 B. J. Kemp, personal communication (to

be published in *Cambridge History of Africa*, Volume I).
21 Säve-Söderbergh 1941: 27.
22 Säve-Söderbergh 1941: 30–36; O'Connor, personal communication.
23 Engelbach 1938.
24 Simpson 1963a: 50–53.

CHAPTER IV

1 Bietak 1968: 93–98.
2 Bietak 1966: 31–38.
3 Steindorff 1935: 202–19.
4 Adams 1975.
5 Arkell 1961: 49–53; Edel 1967.
6 Gratien 1974.
7 Nordström 1966. For traits other than pottery that may embrace all or part of this horizon, see Huard 1967–68.
8 Arkell 1954.
9 Bietak 1966: 38–42.
10 Bietak 1968: 133–35; O'Connor 1974: 29–30.
11 Goedicke (1960) interprets this title to mean 'Overseer of foreign (mercenaries)' and is followed in this by Kadish 1966: 24.
12 Säve-Söderbergh 1941: 14. For a translation of relevant parts of the text, see Gardiner 1961: 94–96.
13 Gardiner 1961: 103.
14 Säve-Söderbergh 1941: 11.
15 Concerning the route to Punt, cf. Kitchen 1971.
16 Säve-Söderbergh 1941: 27–29.
17 Trigger 1965: 82.
18 Edel 1955; see also Dixon 1958.
19 Priese 1974.
20 Priese 1973.
21 Säve-Söderbergh 1941: 106–8.
22 Kadish 1966.

23 Säve-Söderbergh 1941: 11.
24 Frankfort 1956: 121–37.
25 For dissent, see Kees 1961: 312; Kadish 1966: 32, n. 7.
26 Säve-Söderbergh 1941: 29.
27 Bell 1971.
28 O'Connor 1974: 27.
29 Säve-Söderbergh 1941: 50–53.
30 Fischer 1961.
31 Junker 1920.
32 O'Connor 1974: 27–28.
33 Vercoutter 1957: 69; for context, see Bell 1971: 8–9.
34 Säve-Söderbergh 1941: 45.
35 Säve-Söderbergh 1941: 43–44; 46–50; O'Connor 1974: 30.
36 Hayes 1971: 485.
37 O'Connor 1974: 30.
38 Säve-Söderbergh 1941: 60–61; Fischer 1964: 112–18; Habachi 1963.
39 Säve-Söderbergh 1941: 58–60.
40 Säve-Söderbergh 1941: 57.
41 H. Smith 1972.
42 Hayes 1971: 487.

CHAPTER V

1 Säve-Söderbergh 1941: 64; for text, see Lichtheim 1973: 143.
2 Simpson 1963b.
3 Engelbach 1933; however, the inscription may be posthumous.
4 Säve-Söderbergh 1941: 69–70.
5 Säve-Söderbergh 1941: 30–36.
6 H. Smith 1966b: 231–32.
7 Säve-Söderbergh 1941: 67–69.
8 Säve-Söderbergh 1941: 70–71.
9 Posener 1958.
10 Säve-Söderbergh 1941: 72.
11 Säve-Söderbergh 1941: 73.
12 Lucas 1948: 236.

13 Vercoutter 1959: 133–35.
14 Hayes 1971: 505–6.
15 Säve-Söderbergh 1941: 75.
16 For a discussion of meaning of the adjective ḥsy as 'defeated' rather than 'vile', see Lorton 1973.
17 Säve-Söderbergh 1941: 76.
18 Säve-Söderbergh 1941: 76–78; Vercoutter 1966: 164.
19 Säve-Söderbergh 1941: 103.
20 Säve-Söderbergh 1941: 84–85; H. Smith 1966b: 228–29.
21 Lawrence 1965.
22 Säve-Söderbergh 1941: 33. O'Connor (1974: 28) indicates that the remains of one such fortification may be known from Edfu.
23 Adams 1975; for similar estimates, see Vila 1970b: 198–99.
24 Trigger 1965: 160.
25 Adams 1975.
26 Vercoutter 1957.
27 Vila 1970a: 204–14.
28 Vila 1970b.
29 Dunham and Janssen 1960; for names of forts, see Gardiner 1916.
30 Zabkar 1972.
31 Dunham 1967; Badawy 1964.
32 Säve-Söderbergh 1941: 76; Vercoutter 1970: 187.
33 Ruby 1964.
34 Adams 1975.
35 Adams 1975.
36 Priese 1974; Posener 1940: 48–54.
37 Säve-Söderbergh 1941: 77–78; for text, see Lichtheim 1973: 118–20.
38 Knudstad 1966: 176–77.
39 Griffith 1921: 80–83.
40 Simpson 1963a: 50.
41 Bietak 1968: 98–105.

Notes on the Text

42 Säve-Söderbergh 1963b: 58.
43 Adams 1975.
44 Säve-Söderbergh 1941: 74.
45 Nordström 1962: 40–41.
46 O'Connor 1974: 30; Bietak 1968: 135.
47 Trigger 1965: 160.
48 Trigger 1965: 99.

CHAPTER VI

1 Bell 1975: 238.
2 Badawy 1964: 52.
3 Vercoutter 1966.
4 Hesse 1970: 51–67; Bell 1975: 232–35.
5 Hayes 1973a: 52–53.
6 Säve-Söderbergh 1941: 119.
7 Leclant 1973: 429; Säve-Söderbergh 1941: 119–20.
8 Smither 1945.
9 Emery 1965: 102.
10 Arkell 1961: 54.
11 Emery 1965: 102; 167.
12 Adams 1975.
13 Reisner 1910: 342.
14 Reisner 1923a: 21–40.
15 Junker 1921.
16 Hintze 1964.
17 Adams 1975.
18 Junker 1932.
19 Adams 1975.
20 Reisner 1923a: 61–121; Reisner 1923b: 3–21.
21 Säve-Söderbergh 1941: 110–14.
22 O'Connor 1974: 31–32.
23 Adams 1975.
24 O'Connor 1971: 7.
25 Mills and Nordström 1966: 7–11; Adams 1975.
26 Vercoutter 1958; Gratien 1973; 1974.
27 Säve-Söderbergh 1956: 59.

28 Säve-Söderbergh 1941: 124–26; Hayes 1973a: 59–61.
29 Hayes 1973a: 60–61.
30 Säve-Söderbergh 1941: 141.
31 Vercoutter 1970: 183–84.
32 Säve-Söderbergh 1949: 55.
33 Säve-Söderbergh 1949: 50–54.
34 Mills and Nordström 1966: 10–11; Adams and Nordström 1963: 19–21.
35 Bietak 1968: 123, 154.
36 Trigger 1965: 160; Säve-Söderbergh 1941: 129.
37 Bietak 1968: 149–53.
38 Bietak 1968: 112.
39 Sauneron 1965.
40 Randall-MacIver and Woolley 1909: 5–18.
41 Steindorff 1937: 35.
42 Steindorff 1935: 214–15.
43 Säve-Söderbergh 1963b: 58.

CHAPTER VII

1 Habachi 1972; Hayes 1973a: 62–63.
2 Simpson 1963a: 34.
3 Bietak 1966: 43–78.
4 For the date of Cemetery D from Toshka West, which has wrongly been dated as early as the Middle Kingdom, see Trigger 1968: 191–92.
5 Bietak 1966: 65–70.
6 Reisner 1920; Säve-Söderbergh 1941: 144.
7 Säve-Söderbergh 1941: 145–46.
8 Säve-Söderbergh 1941: 146.
9 Hintze 1964: 85.
10 Säve-Söderbergh 1941: 146–50; Arkell 1950: 36–39.
11 Vercoutter 1959: 135.
12 Arkell 1961: 85.
13 Säve-Söderbergh 1941: 150–52.

14 Redford 1967: 57–59; 61.
15 Säve-Söderbergh 1941: 155.
16 On Syrian industry, see Drower 1973: 510–15.
17 Wild 1959: 86–87.
18 Priese 1974.
19 Hayes 1973b: 348–49; Säve-Söderbergh 1941: 175–84.
20 Säve-Söderbergh 1941: 206–26.
21 Säve-Söderbergh 1941: 156–59; 228.
22 Säve-Söderbergh 1941: 168; Fairman 1948: 8.
23 Säve-Söderbergh 1941: 227; Priese 1974.
24 Säve-Söderbergh 1941: 226–27.
25 Säve-Söderbergh 1941: 210–11.
26 Vercoutter 1959: 140–42; Säve-Söderbergh 1941: 188.
27 Mills 1965: 7.
28 Säve-Söderbergh 1941: 188.
29 Piotrovsky 1967.
30 Priese 1974.
31 Priese 1974; Säve-Söderbergh 1941: 185; 228.
32 Simpson 1963a: 26.
33 Säve-Söderbergh 1960.
34 Säve-Söderbergh 1963a.
35 Simpson 1963a: 11.
36 Davies and Gardiner 1926.
37 Säve-Söderbergh 1941: 187.
38 Säve-Söderbergh 1941: 159.
39 Simpson 1963a: 36–43, Pl. XXII.
40 Kees 1961: 208.
41 Säve-Söderbergh 1941: 200–5.
42 Emery 1965: 182.
43 Säve-Söderbergh 1941: 189–92.
44 Trigger 1965: 109.
45 Griffith 1921. I am grateful to Professor K. Michalowski for information concerning his recent excavations at Faras and the provenance of the Pharaonic stone blocks found there.

46 Trigger 1965: 109.
47 Säve-Söderbergh 1941: 193; Venot 1974.
48 Säve-Söderbergh 1941: 193.
49 Trigger 1965: 109–10.
50 For summary descriptions of the temples of Egyptian Nubia, see Curto 1966.
51 Caminos 1968.
52 Emery 1965: 194–200.
53 Emery 1965: 200–2; Säve-Söderbergh 1941: 196–97.
54 Emery 1965: 197.
55 Gardiner 1961: 270.
56 Säve-Söderbergh 1941: 168.
57 Kemp 1972.
58 Fairman 1938; 1939; 1948.
59 Vercoutter 1974.
60 Giorgini 1971: 98; Adams 1975.
61 Fairman 1938.
62 Maystre 1967–68; Jacquet-Gordon, Bonnet, and Jacquet 1969.
63 Macadam 1949: xii.
64 Dunham 1970.
65 Säve-Söderbergh 1941: 156.
66 Arkell 1961: 112.
67 See, e.g., the Gebel Agg relief, *supra*.
68 Arkell 1961: 104.
69 Säve-Söderbergh 1941: 199–200.
70 Hayes 1973b: 374.
71 Säve-Söderbergh 1941: 199.
72 Säve-Söderbergh 1941: 199.
73 Edward Wente, personal communication. The inscription is published in Bakir 1952.
74 Trigger 1965: 112.
75 Adams 1964: 105.
76 Säve-Söderbergh 1964: 31.
77 Cf. Emery 1965: 178–79 and Adams 1975.
78 Firth 1927: 25–28.
79 Adams 1964: 106–7.

Notes on the Text

80 Vagn Nielsen 1970: 86–87; cf. Batrawi 1946: 144–45.
81 Mukherjee, Rao, and Trevor 1955: 85.
82 Säve-Söderbergh 1967–68.
83 Adams 1975.
84 Adams 1975.
85 Adams 1964: 106, n. 1.
86 Firth 1927: 28.
87 Butzer 1971: 338–39.
88 Firth 1912: I, 29.
89 Steindorff 1937: 241.
90 Emery 1965: 205–6.
91 Knudstad 1966: 186.
92 Vercoutter 1959: 137; 151.

CHAPTER VIII

1 Säve-Söderbergh 1941: 241–45; concerning economic relations between Egypt and Nubia under Ramesses XI, see Kitchen 1973: 247–48. The latter work is followed extensively for the general history of Egypt in the period covered by this chapter.
2 Wente 1973.
3 Kitchen 1973: 247.
4 Gardiner 1961: 313; Kitchen 1973: 253.
5 Dixon 1964: 131.
6 Arkell 1961: 112–13; Emery 1965: 206–7.
7 Goedicke 1972.
8 Kitchen 1973: 293, 296.
9 Dunham 1950.
10 Priese 1968: 188–89.
11 Arkell 1961: 114, n. 1.
12 Priese 1973.
13 Dunham 1950: 118–20.
14 Dunham 1963.
15 Kitchen 1973: 151.
16 Adams 1975.
17 Shinnie 1967: 73.
18 Griffith 1922: 67–124.
19 Trigger 1965: 112; Adams 1975.
20 Griffith 1923; Adams 1975.
21 Dunham 1950: 110–17.

Bibliography

The most comprehensive and up to date survey of Nubian culture history is Adams 1975; although for written sources Säve-Söderbergh 1941 remains unchallenged. Briefer surveys include Arkell 1961; Fairservis 1962; Emery 1965; Curto 1966; and Hintze and Hintze 1967. Equally comprehensive but more specialized are Hofmann 1967 and Trigger 1965. Among the more important works dealing with the Unesco Nubian campaign are Gerster 1964; Greener 1962; Keating 1975.

ABBREVIATIONS

AJA   *American Journal of Archaeology*

ASAE   *Annales du Service des Antiquités de l'Egypte*

AWW-phk   Akademie der Wissenschaften in Wien, Philosophisch-historische Klasse

CAH   *Cambridge Ancient History* (Third Edition)

CRIPE   *Cahier de Recherches de l'Institut de Papyrologie et d'Egyptologie de Lille*

EES   Egypt Exploration Society

HAS   *Harvard African Studies*

JARCE   *Journal of the American Research Center in Egypt*

JEA   *Journal of Egyptian Archaeology*

LAAA   *Liverpool Annals of Archaeology and Anthropology*

OAW-phk   Österreichische Akademie der Wissenschaften, Philosophisch-historische Klasse

Or.   *Orientalia*

SJESN   The Scandinavian Joint Expedition to Sudanese Nubia

WA   *World Archaeology*

ZAS   *Zeitschrift für ägyptische Sprache und Altertumskunde*

ADAMS, WILLIAM Y. Post-Pharaonic Nubia in the Light of Archaeology, I. *JEA* 50 (1964), 102–20.
— *Nubia: Corridor to Africa.* London, 1975.
ADAMS, WILLIAM Y. and NORDSTRÖM, H-A. The Archaeological Survey on the West Bank of the Nile: Third Season, 1961–1962. *Kush* 11 (1963), 10–46.

ANDERSON, JAMES E. Late Paleolithic Skeletal Remains from Nubia. *The Prehistory of Nubia.* F. Wendorf (ed.), Volume II: 996–1040. Dallas, 1968.
ARKELL, A. J. *Early Khartoum.* London, 1949.
— Varia Sudanica. *JEA* 36 (1950), 24–40.
— *Shaheinab.* London, 1953.

Bibliography

— Four Occupation Sites at Agordat. *Kush* 2 (1954), 33–62.

— *A History of the Sudan to 1821* (Second Edition). London, 1961.

BADAWY, A. Preliminary Report on the Excavations by the University of California at Askut. *Kush* 12 (1964), 47–53.

BAKIR, A. E. Slavery in Pharaonic Egypt. *ASAE* Supplement 18. Cairo, 1952.

BARBOUR, K. M. *The Republic of the Sudan: A Regional Geography.* London, 1961.

BATRAWI, AHMED. The Racial History of Egypt and Nubia. *Journal of the Royal Anthropological Institute* 75 (1945–46), 81–101; 76: 131–56.

BELL, BARBARA. The Oldest Records of the Nile Floods. *Geographical Journal* 136 (1970), 569–73.

— The Dark Ages in Ancient History. I. The First Dark Age in Egypt. *AJA* 75 (1971), 1–26.

— Climate and the History of Egypt: The Middle Kingdom. *AJA* (1975), 223–69. I.

BIETAK, MANFRED. Ausgrabungen in Sayala⁄Nubien 1961–1965: Denkmäler der C⁄Gruppe und der Pan⁄Gräber⁄Kultur. *OAW⁄phk*, Denkschriften 92. Vienna, 1966.

— Studien zur Chronologie der Nubischen C⁄Gruppe. *OAW⁄phk*, Denkschriften 97. Vienna, 1968.

BIETAK, MANFRED and ENGELMAYER, R. Eine frühdynastische Abri⁄Siedlung mit Felsbildern aus Sayala⁄Nubien. *OAW⁄phk*, Denkschriften 82. Vienna, 1963.

BUTZER, KARL W. *Environment and Archeology* (Second Edition). Chicago, 1971.

BUTZER, KARL W. and HANSEN, C.L. *Desert and River in Nubia.* Madison, 1968.

CAMINOS, R. A. *The Shrines and Rock⁄Inscrip-*

tions of Ibrim. EES, Archaeological Survey of Egypt, Memoir 32. London, 1968.

CARLSON, R. L. and SIGSTAD, J. S. Paleo⁄lithic and Late Neolithic Sites Excavated by the Fourth Colorado Expedition. *Kush* 15 (1967–68), 51–58.

CHRISTOPHE, L. A. Remarques sur l'économie de la Basse⁄Nubie égyptienne. *Bulletin de la Société de Géographie d'Egypte* 35 (1963), 77–128.

CHURCHER, C. S. *Late Pleistocene Vertebrates from Archaeological Sites in the Plain of Kom Ombo, Upper Egypt.* Royal Ontario Museum, Life Sciences Contributions, 82. Toronto, 1972.

CLARK, J. DESMOND. *The Prehistory of Africa.* London, 1970.

— A Re⁄examination of the Evidence for Agricultural Origins in the Nile Valley. *Proceedings of the Prehistoric Society* 37 (1971), 34–79.

— 1973. Shabona. *Nyame Akuma* 3 (1973), 60–64.

CURTO, S. *Nubien.* Munich, 1966.

DAVIES, N. DE GARIS and GARDINER, A. H. *The Tomb of Huy, Viceroy of Nubia in the Reign of Tutankhamun (No. 40).* EES, Theban Tomb Series, Fourth Memoir. London, 1926.

DE HEINZELIN, JEAN. Geological History of the Nile Valley in Nubia. *The Prehistory of Nubia.* F. Wendorf (ed.), Volume I: 19–55.

DIXON, D. M. The Land of Yam. *JEA* 44 (1958), 40–55.

— The Origin of the Kingdom of Kush. *JEA* 50 (1964), 121–32.

DROWER, MARGARET S. Syria *c.* 1550–1400 BC. *CAH*, Volume II, Part 1: 417–525. Cambridge, 1973.

DUNHAM, DOWS. *The Royal Cemeteries of Kush*, I: *El Kurru*. Boston, 1950.

— *The Royal Cemeteries of Kush*, V: *The West and South Cemeteries at Meroe*. Boston, 1963.

— *Second Cataract Forts*, Volume 2, *Uronarti, Shalfak, Mirgissa*. Boston, 1967.

— *The Barkal Temples*. Boston, 1970.

DUNHAM, D. and JANSSEN, J. M. A. *Second Cataract Forts*, Volume 1, *Semna, Kumma*. Boston, 1960.

EDEL, ELMAR. *Inschriften des alten Reiches*, V, *Die Reiseberichte des Hrw-hwjf (Herchuf)*. Ägyptologische Studien, Otto Firchow (ed.), 1955.

— Die Ländernamen Unternubiens und die Ausbreitung der C-Gruppe nach den Reiseberichten des Hrw-hwjf. *Or.* 36 (1967), 133–58.

EDWARDS, I. E. S. The Early Dynastic Period in Egypt. *CAH*, Volume I, Part 2: 1–70. Cambridge, 1971.

EMERY, WALTER B. *Archaic Egypt*. Harmondsworth, 1961.

— Egypt Exploration Society: Preliminary Report on the Excavations at Buhen, 1962. *Kush* 11 (1963), 116–20.

— *Egypt in Nubia*. London, 1965.

EMERY, W. B. and KIRWAN, L. P. *The Excavations and Survey Between Wadi es-Sebua and Adindan*. (2 volumes). Cairo, 1935.

ENGELBACH, R. The Quarries of the Western Nubian Desert: A Preliminary Report. *ASAE* 33 (1933), 65–74.

— The Quarries of the Western Nubian Desert and the Ancient Road to Tushka. *ASAE* 38 (1938), 369–90.

FAIRMAN, H. W. Preliminary Report on the Excavations at Sesebi (Sudla) and Amarah West, Anglo-Egyptian Sudan 1937–8. *JEA* 24 (1938), 151–56.

— Preliminary Report on the Excavations at Amarah West, Anglo-Egyptian Sudan, 1938–9. *JEA* 25 (1939), 139–44.

— Preliminary Report on the Excavations at Amarah West, Anglo-Egyptian Sudan. *JEA* 34 (1948), 3–11.

FAIRSERVIS, WALTER A. *The Ancient Kingdoms of the Nile*. New York, 1962.

FIRTH, C. M. *The Archaeological Survey of Nubia, Report for 1908–1909* (2 volumes). Cairo, 1912.

— *The Archaeological Survey of Nubia, Report for 1909–1910*. Cairo, 1915.

— *The Archaeological Survey of Nubia, Report for 1910–1911*. Cairo, 1927.

FISCHER, HENRY G. The Nubian Mercenaries of Gebelein during the First Intermediate Period. *Kush* 9 (1961), 44–80.

— *Inscriptions from the Coptite Nome, Dynasties VI–XI*. Analecta Orientalia 40. Rome, 1964.

FRANKFORT, HENRI. *The Birth of Civilization in the Near East*. New York, 1956.

GARDINER, ALAN. An Ancient List of the Fortresses of Nubia. *JEA* 3 (1916), 184–92.

— *Egypt of the Pharaohs*. Oxford, 1961.

GERSTER, G. *Nubien: Goldland am Nil*. Zürich, 1964.

GIORGINI, M. S. *Soleb*, II, *Les Nécropoles*. Florence, 1971.

GOEDICKE, H. The Title imy-r° in the Old Kingdom. *JEA* 46 (1960), 60–64.

— Review of Dunham *The Barkal Temples*. *AJA* 76 (1972), 89.

GRATIEN, B. *Les Nécropoles Kerma de l'île de Saï*, I. *CRIPE* No. 1 (1973), 143–84 and No. 11 (1974), 143–84.

GREENER, LESLIE. *High Dam Over Nubia*. London, 1962.

Bibliography

GRIFFITH, F. L. Oxford Excavations in Nubia: Nubia from the Old to the New Kingdom. *LAAA* 8 (1921), 65–104.

— Oxford Excavations in Nubia: Napata. *LAAA* 9 (1922), 67–124.

— Oxford Excavations in Nubia: Sanam Cemetery. *LAAA* 10 (1923), 73–171.

HABACHI, LABIB. King Nebhepetre Men-thuhotp: His Monuments, Place in History, Deification and Unusual Representations in the Form of Gods. *Mitteilungen des Deutschen Instituts für ägyptische Altertum-skunde in Kairo* 19 (1963), 16–52.

— *The Second Stela of Kamose, and his Struggle against the Hyksos Ruler and his Capital.* Abhandlungen des Deutschen Archäo-logischen Instituts Abteilung Kairo, Ägyptologische Reihe 8. Glückstadt, 1972.

HAYES, W. C. The Middle Kingdom in Egypt. *CAH*, Volume I, Part 2 (1971), 464–531.

— Egypt from the Death of Ammenemes III to Saqenenre II. *CAH*, Volume II, Part 1 (1973a), 42–76.

— Egypt: Internal Affairs from Tuthmosis I to the Death of Amenophis III. *CAH*, Volume II, Part 1 (1973b), 313–416.

HELCK, W. Zwei Einzelprobleme der thinitischen Chronologie. *Mitteilungen des Deutschen Archäologischen Instituts Abteilung Kairo* 26 (1970), 83–85.

HESSE, A. Introduction géophysique et notes techniques. *Mirgissa I.* (J. Vercoutter, ed.) pp. 51–122. Paris, 1970.

HINTZE, FRITZ. Das Kerma-Problem. *ZAS* 91 (1964), 79–86.

HINTZE, FRITZ and HINTZE, URSULA. *Alte Kulturen im Sudan.* Munich, 1967.

HOFMANN, INGE. *Die Kulturen des Niltals von Aswan bis Sennar.* Hamburg, 1967.

HUARD, PAUL. Influences culturelles trans-mises au Sahara tchadien par le Groupe C de Nubie. *Kush* 15 (1967–68), 84–124.

IBN KHALDUN, ABD AR-RAHMAN. *The Muqad-dimah: An Introduction to History* (F. Rosen-thal, translator; edited and abridged by N. J. Dawood). Princeton, 1967.

JACQUET-GORDON, H., BONNET, C. and JACQUET, J. Pnubs and the Temple of Tabo on Argo Island. *JEA* 55 (1969), 103–11.

JUNKER, HERMANN. *Bericht über die Grabungen auf den Friedhöfen von El-Kubanieh-Süd.* AWW–phk, Denkschriften 62 (3). Vienna, 1919.

— *Bericht über die Grabungen auf den Friedhöfen von El-Kubanieh-Nord.* AWW-phk, Denk-schriften 64 (3). Vienna, 1920.

— *Die nubische Ursprung der sogenannten Tell el-Jahudiye-Vasen.* AWW-phk, Denk-schriften 63. Vienna, 1921.

— *Toshke.* AWW-phk, Denkschriften 68 (1). Vienna, 1926.

— *Bemerkungen zur Kerma-Kunst. Studies Presented to F. Ll. Griffith* (S. R. K. Glanville, ed.), pp. 297–303. London, 1932.

KADISH, GERALD E. Old Kingdom Egyptian Activity in Nubia: Some Reconsiderations. *JEA* 52 (1966), 23–33.

KAISER, WERNER. Einige Bemerkungen zur ägyptischen Frühzeit. *ZAS* 91 (1964), 86–125.

KANTOR, HELENE. The Final Phase of Predynastic Culture: Gerzean or Se-mainean? *Journal of Near Eastern Studies* 3 (1944), 110–36.

KEATING, REX. *Nubian Rescue.* London, 1975.

KEES, HERMANN. *Ancient Egypt: A Cultural Topography.* Chicago, 1961.

KEMP, B. J. The Egyptian 1st Dynasty Royal Cemetery. *Antiquity* 41 (1967), 22–32.

— Fortified Towns in Nubia. *Man, Settlement and Urbanism.* P. J. Ucko, R. Tringham and G. W. Dimbleby (eds.), pp. 651–56. London, 1972.

— Photographs of the Decorated Tomb. *JEA* 59 (1973), 36–43.

KITCHEN, K. A. Punt and how to get there. *Or.* 40 (1971), 184–207.

— *The Third Intermediate Period in Egypt (1100–650 BC).* Warminster, 1973.

KNUDSTAD, JAMES. Serra East and Dorginarti. *Kush* 14 (1966), 165–86.

LAL, B. B. Indian Archaeological Expedition to Nubia, 1962, A Preliminary Report. *Fouilles en Nubie (1961–1963),* pp. 97–118. Cairo, 1967.

LAWRENCE, A. W. Ancient Egyptian Fortifications. *JEA* 51 (1965), 69–94.

LECLANT, JEAN. Fouilles et travaux en Egypte et au Soudan, 1971–72. *Or.* 42 (1973), 393–440.

LICHTHEIM, M. *Ancient Egyptian Literature,* Volume I, *The Old and Middle Kingdoms.* Berkeley, 1973.

LORTON, DAVID. The So-called 'Vile' Enemies of the King of Egypt (in the Middle Kingdom and Dynasty XVIII). *JARCE* 10 (1973), 65–70.

LUCAS, A. *Ancient Egyptian Materials and Industries* (Third Edition). London, 1948.

MACADAM, M. F. L. *The Temples of Kawa, I.* Oxford, 1949.

MARKS, A. E. Survey and Excavations in the Dongola Reach, Sudan. *Current Anthropology* 9 (1968), 319–23.

MARKS, A. E., HAYS T. R. and DE HEINZELIN, J. Preliminary Report of the Southern Methodist University Expedition in the Dongola Reach. *Kush* 15 (1967–68), 165–92.

MAYSTRE, CHARLES. Excavations at Tabo, Argo Island, 1965–1968, Preliminary Report. *Kush* 15 (1967–68), 193–99.

MILLS, A. J. The Reconnaissance Survey from Gemai to Dal: A Preliminary Report for 1963–1964. *Kush* 13 (1965), 1–12.

MILLS, A. J. and NORDSTRÖM, H.-A. The Archaeological Survey from Gemai to Dal. *Kush* 14 (1966), 1–15.

MUKHERJEE, R., RAO, C. R. and TREVOR J. C. *The Ancient Inhabitants of Jebel Moya.* Cambridge, 1955.

NORDSTRÖM, H.-A. Excavations and Survey in Faras, Argin, and Gezira Dabarosa. *Kush* 10 (1962), 34–61.

— A-Group and C-Group in Upper Nubia. *Kush* 14 (1966), 63–68.

— Neolithic and A-Group Sites. *SJESN,* Volume 3. Uppsala, 1972.

O'CONNOR, DAVID. Ancient Egypt and Black Africa – Early Contacts. *Expedition* 14 (1971), 2–9.

— Political Systems and Archaeological Data in Egypt. *WA* 6 (1974), 15–38.

PIOTROVSKY, BORIS. The Early Dynasty Settlement of Khor-Daoud and Wadi-Allaki: the Ancient Route to the Gold Mines. *Fouilles en Nubie (1961–1963),* Service des Antiquités de l'Egypte, pp. 127–40. Cairo, 1967.

POSENER, G. *Princes et Pays d'Asie et de Nubie.* Bruxelles, 1940.

— Pour une localisation du pays Koush au Moyen Empire. *Kush* 6 (1958), 39–68.

PRIESE, K.-H. Nichtägyptische Namen und Wörter in den ägyptischen Inschriften der Könige von Kusch, I. *Mitteilungen des Instituts für Orientforschung der Deutschen*

Bibliography

Akademie der Wissenschaften zur Berlin 14 (2) (1968), 165–91.

— Articula. Etudes et Travaux 7 (1973), 156–62.

— 'rm und '3m, das Land Irame: Ein Beitrag zur Topographie des Sudan im Altertum, Altorientalische forschungen I (1974), 7–41.

RANDALL-MACIVER, D. and WOOLLEY, C. L. Areika. Philadelphia, 1909.

REDFORD, DONALD B. History and Chronology of the Eighteenth Dynasty of Egypt: Seven Studies. Toronto, 1967.

REISNER, GEORGE A. The Archaeological Survey of Nubia, Report for 1907–1908 (2 volumes). Cairo, 1910.

— The Viceroys of Ethiopia. JEA 6 (1920), 28–55; 73–88.

— Excavations at Kerma, I–III. HAS 5. Boston, 1923a.

— Excavations at Kerma, IV–V. HAS 6. Boston, 1923b.

RUBY, J. W. Preliminary Report of the University of California Expedition to Dabnarti, 1963. Kush 12 (1964), 54–56.

SAUNERON, SERGE. Un Village nubien fortifié sur la rive orientale de Ouadi es-Sébou. Bulletin de l'Institut français d'archéologie orientale 63 (1965), 161–67.

SÄVE-SÖDERBERGH, T. Agypten und Nubien: Ein Beitrag zur Geschichte altägyptischer Aussenpolitik. Lund, 1941.

— A Buhen Stela from the Second Intermediate Period. JEA 35 (1949), 50–58.

— The Nubian Kingdom of the Second Intermediate Period. Kush 4 (1956), 54–61.

— The Paintings in the Tomb of Djehutyhetep at Debeira. Kush 8 (1960), 25–44.

— The Tomb of the Prince of Teh-khet, Amenemhet. Kush 11 (1963a), 159–74.

— Preliminary Report of the Scandinavian Joint Expedition, 1961–62. Kush 11 (1963b), 47–69.

— Preliminary Report of the Scandinavian Joint Expedition, 1962–63. Kush 12 (1964), 19–39.

— The Egyptianization and Depopulation of Lower Nubia. Kush 15 (1967–68), 237–42.

SCHILD, R. et al. The Arkinian and Shamarkian Industries. The Prehistory of Nubia. F. Wendorf (ed.), Volume II: 651–767. Dallas, 1968.

SHINER, J. L. The Cataract Tradition. The Prehistory of Nubia. F. Wendorf (ed.), Volume II: 535–629. Dallas, 1968.

SHINNIE, P. L. Meroe. London, 1967.

SIMPSON, WILLIAM K. Heka-nefer and the Dynastic Material from Toshka and Arminna. Publications of the Pennsylvania-Yale Expedition to Egypt, No. 1. New Haven and Philadelphia, 1963a.

— Studies in the Twelfth Egyptian Dynasty, I: The Residence of Itj-towe. JARCE 2 (1963b), 53–59.

SMITH, HARRY S. Preliminary Reports of the Egypt Exploration Society's Nubian Survey. Cairo, 1962.

— The Nubian B-Group. Kush 14 (1966a), 69–124.

— Kor: Report on the Excavations of the Egypt Exploration Society at Kor, 1965. Kush 14 (1966b), 187–243.

— The Rock Inscriptions of Buhen. JEA 58 (1972), 43–82.

SMITH, PHILIP E. L. The Late Paleolithic of Northeast Africa in the Light of Recent Research. American Anthropologist 68 (2), Special Publication, J. D. Clark and F. C. Howell (eds.), 1966. Recent Studies in Paleoanthropology, pp. 326–55.

SMITHER, P. C. The Semnah Despatches. *JEA* 31 (1945), 3–10.

STEINDORFF, GEORG. *Aniba*, Volume 1. Glückstadt, 1935.

— *Aniba*, Volume 2. Glückstadt, 1937.

TRIGGER, BRUCE G. *History and Settlement in Lower Nubia*. Yale University Publications in Anthropology, No. 69. New Haven, 1965.

— Review of Bietak, Ausgrabungen in Sayala-Nubien. *Bibliotheca Orientalis* 25 (1968), 190–92.

— The Archaeology of Government. *WA* 6 (1974), 95–106.

— In press. The Rise of Civilization in Egypt. *Cambridge History of Africa*, Volume I (J. D. Clark, ed.).

VAGN NIELSEN, O. *Human Remains*. SJESN, Volume 9. Uppsala, 1970.

VENOT, C. Le cimetière MX TD de Mirgissa. *CRIPE* No. 2 (1974), 27–49.

VERCOUTTER, JEAN. Upper Egyptian Settlers in Middle Kingdom Nubia. *Kush* 5 (1957), 61–69.

— Excavations at Saï, 1955–57. *Kush* 6 (1958), 144–69.

— The Gold of Kush. *Kush* 7 (1959), 120–53.

— Semna South Fort and the Records of Nile Levels at Kumma. *Kush* 14 (1966), 125–64.

— *Mirgissa I*. Paris, 1970.

— Saï 1972–1973. *CRIPE*, No. 2 (1974), 11–26.

VILA, A. Les Vestiges de la plaine. *Mirgissa I* (J. Vercoutter, ed.). pp. 193–221. Paris, 1970a.

— L'armement de la forteresse de Mirgissa-Iken. *Revue d'Egyptologie* 22 (1970b), 171–99.

WENDORF, F. Late Paleolithic Sites in Egyptian Nubia. *The Prehistory of Nubia*. F. Wendorf (ed.), Volume II: 791–953, Dallas, 1968a.

— Summary of Nubian Prehistory. *The Prehistory of Nubia*. F. Wendorf (ed.), Volume II: 1041–59. Dallas, 1968b.

WENDORF, FRED, SAID, R. and SCHILD, R. Egyptian Prehistory: Some New Concepts. *Science* 169 (1970), 1161–71.

WENDT, W. E. Two Prehistoric Archeological Sites in Egyptian Nubia. *Postilla of the Yale Peabody Museum* No. 102 (1966), 1–46.

WENTE, E. Report on the Work of the Epigraphic Survey of the Oriental Institute, Luxor, Egypt, for the Season 1972–1973. *American Research Center in Egypt, Newsletter* 86 (1973), 30–32.

WILD, HENRI. Une danse nubienne d'époque pharaonique. *Kush* 7 (1959), 76–90.

ZABKAR, L. V. The Egyptian Name of the Fortress of Semna South. *JEA* 58 (1972), 83–90.

Sources of Illustrations

(Plates listed under source)

Staatliche Museen zu Berlin: 27; Museo Civico, Bologna: 46; Museum of Fine Arts, Boston: 17, 22, 23, 24, 26, 30, 31, 32, 33, 34, 35, 36, 37, 38, 39, 56, 57, 71, 72, 73, 74; British Museum: 45, 67; Cairo Museum: 8, 16; Oriental Institute, University of Chicago: 12, 28, 58, 59, 62, 64, 69, 70; Egyptian Exploration Society: 7, 15; Labib Habachi: 42; Friedrich Hinkel: 3; Fritz Hintze: 1; Max Hirmer: 16; Bild-archiv Foto Marburg: 60; Mission archaeo-logique française: 20, 21; Missione Michela Schiff Giorgini: 65, 66; Metropolitan Museum of Art, New York: 47, 53;

University Museum, University of Pennsylvania: 50; Pennsylvania-Yale Expedition to Egypt: 9, 10, 11, 14, 29, 40, 41, 43, 51, 52, 54, 55, 68; SJE (Scandinavian Joint Expedition to Sudanese Nubia): 2, 5, 48, 49; Dr William Kelly Simpson: 19, 25 Egyptian Museum, Turin: 44 Roger Wood: 61, 63.

The cost of preparing or obtaining a substantial number of the illustrations that appear in this book has been covered by a Research Grant from the Faculty of Graduate Studies and Research, McGill University.

166

The Plates

1

2

3

4

5

6

7

8

9

11

10

12

13

14

15

16

17

18

19

20

21

22

24

25

26

27

28

29

30

31

32

33

34

35

36

37

38

39

40

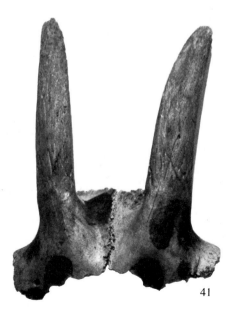

41

42

43

44

45

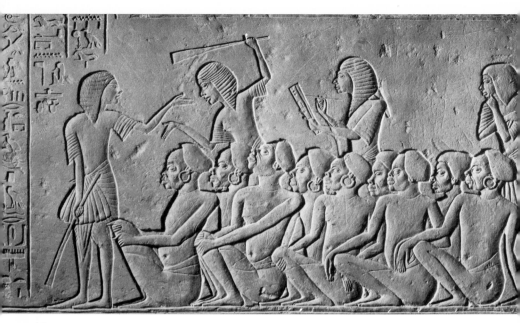

46

47

48

49

50   51

52

53

54

55

57

58

59

60

61

62

63

65

66

67

68

69

70

71

72

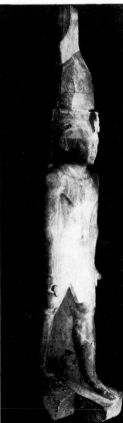

73

Notes on the Plates

1 Rock pictures of giraffes at site 21·X·1 (Kulb in the Batn el·Hagar). Although rock pictures are notoriously difficult to date, on stylistic and associational grounds these have been designated as late pre· historic. Giraffes continue to be represented in Nubia into later times.

2 Terminal A·Group grave (No. 49) from cemetery 401 at Sahaba, north of Wadi Halfa. The body is of a mature male. A leather cap covers the head, an ostrich feather fan the lower part of the chest and part of the arms. Below the fan is a light· grey quartzite palette bearing traces of green malachite pigment. The photograph is taken from the north.

3 Egyptian relief from Gebel Shaikh Sulei· man showing Egyptian ship with prison· ers and slaughtered foes. The attribution of the scene to the reign of King Djer is based on the *serekh* on the far left which Arkell believed contained his name. This in· terpretation has recently been challenged. Nevertheless, the relief indicates Egyptian activity in the vicinity of the Second Cataract about the beginning of the First Dynasty.

4 Terminal A·Group settlement at Afyeh, Lower Nubia. The houses were con· structed of rough sandstone slabs set in Nile mud. Some had as many as six rooms with interconnecting doorways, which may have been provided with single·leaved wooden doors. The lack of similar houses in contemporary A·Group sites suggests that this site may have been the residence of a local chieftain.

5 Bowl of black·mouthed 'egg·shell' ware with red painted design on pale brown background. Nordström's Type A VIII a6. From grave 49, cemetery 401, Sahaba.

6 Recto of the Palermo Stone, a fragment of a black basalt monument providing a record of the early kings of Egypt through the Fifth Dynasty. The top row gives the names of Predynastic rulers. The following rows provide the names of later kings and are divided into compartments, each listing one or more memorable events for each successive year of their reigns. The first substantially preserved compartment in the bottom row is for a year $(X + 2)$ of the reign of Sneferu. Among various activities, in· cluding ship·building, it records 'hacking up the land of the Nubians. Bringing of 7,000 living prisoners and 200,000 large and small cattle'. Height 43.5 cm., width 25 cm., thickness 6.5 cm. Palermo Museum.

7 Buildings of Fourth and Fifth Dynas· ties at Buhen. Part of the Old Kingdom town located north of the later Middle Kingdom Fortress at Buhen. The town had defence walls of rough stone masonry 2 metres wide and the buildings were of a mixture of brick and dry stone walls. The earliest construction at the site may date

from the Third Dynasty or earlier. Various rebuilding went on in the course of the settlement's long history

8 Seated statue showing King Khafre under the protection of the hawk-god Horus. A little over life-size, the statue was found in the Valley Temple of the king's pyramid complex at Giza. The grey-green diorite for the statue probably came from the Toshka quarries, which were already worked by Khafre's predecessor King Khufu. Height 168 cm. Fourth Dynasty, *c.* 2520 BC. Cairo Museum.

9 Weathered sandstone fragment of an Old Kingdom inscription found at Toshka West. The toponym Satju is visible in the first (right-hand) column of text. The second column reads 'I have brought all good things that come therefrom.' It is possible that this stela, like a better pre-served one of the Middle Kingdom found nearby, commemorates the exploitation of the diorite quarries of the Western Desert. Height 25 cm., width 21 cm., thickness 12 cm.

10 C-Group burial No. 76 from Cemetery C at Toshka West. The burial, apparently of a woman, had a plain copper mirror by the head, four ivory rings on the left hand, a necklace of mottled stone and faience beads, and triple-strand anklets of ostrich egg-shell beads. There were also traces of a leather garment. Provisionally attributed to the Middle Kingdom.

11 Pair of ivory armlets from a tomb of the C-Group period. Cemetery C at Toshka West.

12 Entrance to tomb of Harkhuf, in the cliff at Kubbet el-Hawa, opposite Aswan. Har-

khuf is represented on either side of the doorway; on the left he leans on a staff with his son holding a censer in front of him. The biographical inscriptions on either side of the doorway recount his first three trading expeditions to Nubia. Out of sight on the far right is the child king Pepi II's letter concerning the dwarf Harkhuf brought from Nubia on his fourth expedi-tion. Above the entrance are the standard prayers for offerings and a good burial and a listing of the deceased's virtues.

13 Figures from a painted model of a com-pany of forty Nubian archers. Found in the tomb of Mesehti at Assiut, alongside a similar group representing Egyptian spear-men. The Nubians are distinguished by their dark skin and polychrome garments. First Intermediate Period, Tenth Dynasty. Height 35.5 cm. Cairo Museum.

14 Portions of titularies of Kings Kakare-Intef and Iyibkhentre on a rock at Toshka East. These may record efforts by Egyptian rulers of the First Intermediate Period to control Lower Nubia. Although unknown from the surviving evidence in Egypt, these names are attested elsewhere in Lower Nubia.

15 Deeply inscribed Middle Kingdom hier-atic graffito from Buhen. Hill A, No. 6. The text reads: 'Wedjato's son Amenemhet's son Nesmon's son Amen-emhet. The scribe Iwu's son In's son In's son Mentuhotep. Heren's son In's son Kay. Hika's son Itj's son Itj'. These inscriptions appear to date from the Twel-fth Dynasty and the four individuals commemorated may be members of a watch party stationed on the hill. The two

cattle to the left are C-Group in style and somewhat earlier than the hieratic texts.

16 Statue of King Senwosret III. A highly individual portrait from Medamud near Karnak. On the breast an amulet is suspended from a necklace. The arms and sections of the legs are restored. Dark-grey granite. Total height of statue 167.5 cm. Cairo Museum No. 6049.

17 View of the Semna Cataract, looking southeast from the Semna fort. A narrow felsite dike crosses the Nile, forcing the entire flow of the river through a gap that is scarcely more than 30 metres wide during the season of low water. The fortress of Kumma, on the east side of the Cataract, is visible at top left. This photograph was taken in the course of Reisner's excavations at Semna in the 1920s.

18 The fortress at Buhen, showing the northwest line of Middle Kingdom fortifications. The additions that were made when the fort was reconstructed in the New Kingdom have been removed. The massive mud brick walls were streng-thened by bastions and their base protected by a loop-holed parapet overhanging a rock-cut ditch over 6 metres deep. On the outside of the ditch was a glacis sur-mounted by a covered walkway. Located at the foot of the Second Cataract, Buhen was the major link between the frontier forts and Egypt.

19 Upper part of the Lower River Stair at Uronarti. View looking south. The broad Upper Stair ran outside the north face of the north wall of the fort. It led to a platform from which the upper part of the

Lower Stair descended parallel to the north spur wall of the fort for 110 metres before entering a tunnel. It then continued for another 100 metres to the minimum low water level. These stairs assured the garrison of a water supply in time of siege.

20 Portion of the mud slipway on the plain north of Mirgissa. Approximate width 3.50 metres. Attributed to the Middle Kingdom or the Second Intermediate Period, it was used when wetted to haul cargo and perhaps boats around the Kabuka Rapids. The slipway consists of a concave mud track poured between two lines of mud brick. Traces of human footprints and sledge or keel marks were visible in the dried mud.

21 Remains of stone-tipped spears found in room H in the northwest corner of the Upper Fort at Mirgissa. Three adjacent rooms appear to have been used as an armoury. The rooms contained a large number of flint-tipped spears, javelins, and arrows, as well as bows and shields. The flint was imported from Upper Egypt. The weapons appear to date from the Thirteenth Dynasty. Total length of spears 75–85 cm.

22 Middle Kingdom fort at Semna. View of the north gate looking south over the glacis. The Nile can be seen on the left. The temple of Thutmose III dominates the skyline within the fort. Originally the walls of the fort rose to a height of 10 metres or more.

23 East half of the fortress of Kumma, looking to the southeast (up the Nile). After Reisner's excavations in the 1920s. The

fortress was built on a rocky hill and was small and approximately rectangular. Sections of the outer wall are preserved. Kumma was built in the Twelfth Dynasty but lacks the reconstruction work visible at Semna. During the New Kingdom, it appears to have been occupied only by a small civil community and by priests of a temple dedicated to Khnum and Senwosret III.

24 Southeast wing of the fort at Uronarti, looking southeast. The fort was built on a rocky eminence which it commanded by means of two spur walls. The shorter spur wall, shown here, ran out from the southeast corner of the fort to the southeast, then turned at a right angle. The fort was constructed by Senwosret III in his 16th regnal year.

25 East wall of the Upper Fort at Mirgissa looking north. Just south of the stairway a gate 2.5 metres wide passes through the east wall, giving access to a river stair which descends the cliff to the plain and the river. Traces of buttresses are visible along the outside of the east wall.

26 Upper Fort, Mirgissa. Rostrum in room 32, looking northeast. Room 32 appears originally to have been a long north-south room (24.5 by 7.5 metres) in a block of rooms against the north wall of the inner fort. Against the north wall was a rostrum, stage, or altar of mud brick plastered and painted dark blue. A track worn by footsteps ascending the stair was clearly visible. The three northernmost column bases in room 32 are in contact with the rostrum. One still has the lower part of its wooden column preserved. Beyond, a

portion of the walls of the fort are visible.

27 Red granite stela found at Semna and dating from the sixteenth regnal year of Senwosret III. The round top is filled with the representation of a winged sun disc, below which are 21 lines of text. The text reaffirms Senwosret's establishment of his southern boundary at Heh (Semna) and enjoins his successors to maintain this boundary. It also refers to a statue of himself that Senwosret erected at this point. The stela was discovered by Lepsius in 1844. It was broken into two pieces. Although the lower part was sent immediately to Berlin, the upper part was forgotten by Lepsius' workmen and did not leave Semna until 1886. The two pieces were rejoined in Berlin in 1899. Berlin Museum No. 1157.

28 Middle Kingdom fortress at Serra East. View from upper terrace looking west towards the Nile. The southern half of the interior harbour of the fort is visible at the top of the photograph. The harbour was cut from bedrock, but brick and stone embankments were necessary on all four sides. The proximity of a railway embankment prevented examination of the harbour's connection to the Nile which lay just beyond.

29 Sandstone stela from Toshka West recording work carried out at the diorite quarries in the Western Desert in the fourth regnal year of Amenemhet II. Simpson translates the five vertical lines of text as follows: 'There came the reporter Horemhet to fetch mḫnmt-stone. The number of his force: guardsmen . . .; chamber officials 20; lapidaries 50; quarriers 200; workmen

1,006; asses 1,000'. Height 57.5 cm., width 37 cm., thickness 12–15 cm.

30 Two flood level records from the second and third regnal years of Sekhemre Khut-owe of the Thirteenth Dynasty. These occur on the north face of a granite block near the southeast corner of the Semna fort. The lower inscription states that it was made when the royal treasurer and overseer of the troops, Renseneb, was commander in the fortress of Semna.

31 Western Deffufa at Kerma viewed from the west. The stairway leading to the top of this otherwise solid mud brick structure is clearly visible near the south end. The main part of the Deffufa, visible in this photograph is 52 metres long, 26 metres wide, and still stands 19 metres high. It has been variously interpreted as an Egyptian fort or trading post or part of the palace of the King of Kush.

32 Pottery from burial K 335, Kerma. This was one of the subsidiary graves in Tumu-lus K III. Most of the vessels are Kerma Ware beakers. The photograph indicates the lustrous finish, thin walls, and sharp rims that are characteristic of this ware. Also characteristic is the irregular strip of metallic white separating the black interior lip from the deep red lower portions of these vessels. Contrary to former belief, these vessels were not wheel-made.

33 Daggers and sheaths from Kerma. Dag-gers were very common in the Eastern Cemetery at Kerma. Each consisted of three parts: a blade of bronze, grip of tortoise-shell or wood, and butt of ivory, fastened together with bronze rivets. The blades were from 12 cm. to 42 cm. long. These daggers were distinct local variants of standard Egyptian types. The sheaths generally consist of a single piece of leather, folded lengthwise and sewn down the middle of the back.

34 Ivory-inlaid footboard of bed from Eastern Cemetery at Kerma. The bed was for the main interment in K 449, a subsidiary grave in tumulus K IV. The top row shows four flying vultures with outspread wings, the middle row five Thoeris-figures, and the bottom row four ant-bears. While comparative material from Egypt is largely wanting, the arrangement of the figures appears to be non-Egyptian, although the motifs are Egyptian ones. Length, 65.5 cm.

35 Buttress walls supporting the south wall of the main corridor through tumulus K X, Kerma. View looking east. The careful stepping of the ends of these short walls indicates that they were never intended to extend farther.

36 Tumulus K III in the Eastern Cemetery at Kerma. View looking north after exca-vation. The mortuary chapel known as the Eastern Deffufa (K II) is visible in the background. K III was the largest of the Kerma tumuli, being 90 metres in diam-eter. The framework of the mound con-sisted of a complicated series of mud brick retaining walls, of which some of the lateral ones are here visible. The chambers formed by erecting further short walls between the retaining walls mark subsidiary graves.

37 Life-size statue of the Lady Sennuwy found in the main corridor of K III. Fragments of a companion statue repre-

senting her husband Djefaihapi, Prince of Assiut in Middle Egypt, were also found in the tumulus. Djefaihapi lived in the reign of Senwosret I and the discovery of these statues led Reisner to conclude that he had come south as an Egyptian governor and been buried at Kerma. O'Connor suggests that these statues may have been later gifts from Hyksos kings to their Kushite trading partners. Dark grey granite. Height, 168 cm. Boston, Museum of Fine Arts.

38 Tumulus K IV in the Eastern Cemetery at Kerma. View looking east along the central corridor after excavations. The circular nature of the mound and the arrangement of lateral walls at right angles to the central corridor are plainly visible. The large block of quartzite in the central corridor is the cone that was originally placed on top of the mound. The main burial chamber (A) opened off the south side of the central corridor near the middle. Diameter of mound, 84.5 metres

39 Sacrificial chamber in tumulus K XVIII, Kerma. View looking south. Although K XVIII was not one of the largest or most elaborate of the major tumuli in the Eastern Cemetery, forty-one bodies were distinguished. At the southern end was a trench extending the width of the room, believed by Reisner to have once contained the bed burial(s) of the principal sacrifice(s). The principal burial is thought to have been in the larger adjoining chamber (on the left of the photo). Average length of sacrificial chamber 1252 cm., average width 540 cm.

40 Tomb of the late C-Group, at Toshka East. The burial chamber is in the form of a mud brick vault. The superstructure consisted of a stone ring, originally filled with sand and gravel. Vaulted brick burial chambers occur in Bietak's C-Group period IIb, which is contemporary with the Second Intermediate Period.

41 Gazelle skull daubed with red and black paint, from the Pan-Grave cemetery (TW-D) at Toshka West. Such offerings were often placed alongside the shallow mounds covering Pan-Grave interments.

42 Stela of Kamose. Found in the temple of Karnak in 1954, this is apparently the second of two stelae which described Kamose's war against the Hyksos. The first stela is known from a few broken fragments and from a hieratic copy called the Carnarvon Tablet. The preserved stela records the capture of a letter that the Hyksos king was sending to the ruler of Kush. The stela was erected by the treasurer Neshi, who governed Thebes in the king's absence. Neshi is portrayed at the bottom left of the stela.

43 Bronze dagger found near the offering niche of the principal interment in a small Pan-Grave cemetery (TW-D) at Toshka West. The ivory butt is missing but is sketched in on the basis of other finds. The bronze rivets and wooden inlays of the grip are largely intact. The dagger is of Egyptian not Kerma design, and the cemetery probably dates near the beginning of the Eighteenth Dynasty. The cemetery may belong to a small troop of Medjay who were stationed as part of the Egyptian occupation force in this region early in the New Kingdom.

44 Thutmose I, Conqueror of Upper Nubia. Black granite seated statue in good state of preservation. The king's bare feet rest on nine bows, typifying his supremacy over foreign peoples. Found at Thebes early in the nineteenth century. Height 168 cm. Drovetti Collection, Turin Museum. Catalogue No. 1374.

45 Nubians attacked by Ramesses II from his chariot. This relief from the temple at Beit el-Wali is reproduced from coloured casts by Joseph Bonomi, now in the British Museum. The Nubians are dressed in skins and armed with bows. They retreat to their village which lies among the dom palms. As in many other New Kingdom reliefs, some Nubians are portrayed with brown, others with black skin.

46 Relief showing Nubian captives from the Memphite tomb of General (later King) Horemheb. This finely executed scene shows prisoners being kept under close watch by stick-wielding Egyptian guards, while a scribe records them. Reign of Tutankhamen. Bologna, Museo Civico.

47 Nubian prisoners sent as taxes to Egypt. From the presentation scene in the Theban tomb (No. 40) of Huy, Viceroy of Kush in the reign of Tutankhamen. The five men are attired in skin loincloths. One of the women carries a child on her back and each leads a child by the hand.

48 Pyramid covering tomb of Amenemhet, Prince of Tehkhet, at Debeira West. View looking east towards the Nile. The tomb is cut from a rocky eminence about 300 metres from the Nile. The burial shaft lay directly underneath the pyramid, which

was a little less than 7 metres square and was surrounded by a brick wall. The funerary chapel and a forecourt were cut into the hillside to the southwest of the pyramid.

49 Funerary stela of Amenemhet, Prince of Tehkhet, from the chapel of his tomb at Debeira West. Of grey granite or greywacke. The front surface is well polished and the upper part of the stela is decorated with a relief. On the left, Amenemhet is shown offering a libation to his deceased father Rwiw, Prince of Tehkhet, and to his mother Rwn3. To the right, Amenemhet's wife Hatshepsut offers a drink to her husband and herself; perhaps evidence that Amenemhet died without an heir. The Nubian names of the older generation contrast with the Egyptian ones of the younger generation. Amenemhet appears to have succeeded his brother as Prince of Tehkhet. Dimensions of stela 107 × 68 × 14 cm.

50 Finer of two statues of Amenemhet found at Buhen. The inscription on his arm identifies him as 'the scribe Amenemhet'. A smaller statue found almost touching this one was inscribed as belonging to 'the scribe Amenemhet, begotten of the Prince of Tehket *Rwiw* and his wife *Rwn3*'. Both appear to date prior to Amenemhet himself becoming Prince of Tehkhet. Nothing in the iconography or text of the statue portrayed here indicates Amenemhet's Nubian origin. Many other 'Egyptian' officials in Nubia may have been of similar origin. Of 'hard stone resembling diorite'. Height 36 cm. University Museum 10980.

51 Three rock-cut tombs at Toshka East as seen from the west (river side). They are cut into a sandstone outcrop that has since been eroded by the wind and used as a quarry. On the desert side, the upper half of the hill has been largely cut away. The tomb on the extreme right is that of Hekanefer. The other tombs are uninscribed, but presumably belonged to other Princes of Miam. All date from the New Kingdom.

52 The second chamber in the tomb of Hekanefer at Toshka East. Seen from the southeast. Four pillars supported the roof, but of the southeast pillar only the stump remains. The pit, which is alongside the south wall gives access to the subterranean burial chambers. The chamber is roughly hewn and the corners rounded. Not long after Nubia's conversion to Christianity, this chamber appears to have served as an anchorite's grotto.

53 Nubian nobility as portrayed in the Theban tomb of Huy (No. 40). This presentation scene shows upper class Nubians wearing fashionable Egyptian clothing decorated with ethnic trappings. In the upper left, a Nubian lady rides in an Egyptian chariot pulled by two small oxen. The prince at the upper right is identified as Hekanefer, Prince of Miam. The payments that the Nubians bring to Huy and the king include gold rings, a giraffe, bows, and wooden furniture. Late Eighteenth Dynasty, reign of Tutankhamen.

54 Rock shrine in a partly natural, partly man-made concavity on the side of Gebel Agg at Toshka East. View from south-

west. While the earliest graffito may be of the late Middle Kingdom, the principal cult scenes date from the New Kingdom (late Eighteenth Dynasty). Fragments of a stela and offering basin were found scattered below the shrine. A thick deposit of Pan-Grave pottery and animal bone, also below the shrine, suggests that during the New Kingdom it was a cult centre of the Pan-Grave people.

55 Smoothed panel of natural rock with well carved relief from the rock shrine at Gebel Agg. New Kingdom; probably late Eighteenth Dynasty. 115 cm. long by 42 cm. wide. The panel portrays three seated gods on the right facing a procession of five Nubian worshippers. The gods are Horus Lord of Miam, the deified Senwosret III, and the Syrian god Reshep. The first two worshippers are Nebsy and his wife Tibiw. The third figure is Nebsy's son Humay 'the Medjay of His Majesty' who had the scene cut. Fourth is Humay's brother Seninefer 'the herdsman of the cattle of Horus, Lord of Miam.' The fifth figure is a 'henchman of His Majesty' and also a 'herdsman'. The scene may commemorate an affluent Pan-Grave family of the early New Kingdom.

56 Relief on the exterior of the New Kingdom temple at Semna. It shows the deified Pharaoh Senwosret III, of the Middle Kingdom, embracing Thutmose III, who lived four centuries later and built the temple at Semna. During the New Kingdom, Senwosret III was worshipped as a patron deity in Lower Nubia.

57 Temple of Thutmose III in the fort at Semna. West side, looking east. This

temple is of sandstone and was built or finished by Thutmose III. It consists of one long chamber, still completely roofed. The east portico has three square pillars. The west portico (shown here) retains a rec-tangular pillar at its south end and a polygonal column farther north. The north end of the temple is an addition con-structed of smaller blocks and not bonded to the main structure. The temple is finely decorated.

58 Temple at Amada, viewed from the south. In the foreground is a stone portal which was originally flanked by brick pylons. On the right side of the doorway appears Thutmose III, on the left Amenhotep II, in the presence of Re-Horakhte. These two Pharaohs erected the temple, which was extended by Thutmose IV. The temple was dedicated to Amon-Re and Re-Horakhte. An inscription within the temple recounts that Amenhotep II caused the body of a captured Syrian prince to be hanged on the walls of Napata.

59 Stela of Thutmose III on the façade of his rock-cut shrine or temple at Ellesiya. The inscription is attributed to the fifty-second year of his reign. The temple consisted of two small chambers cut into the rock adjoining a forecourt partly cut from the rock and partly walled in. Wooden beams let into holes in the cliff face supported a roof over the latter chamber. Ellesiya is important as being an early prototype for later rock-cut temples, such as those at Abu Simbel.

60 Façade of the Great Temple hewn into the cliffs on the west bank of the Nile at Abu Simbel. Viewed from the northeast. Each

side of the entrance is flanked by two seated statues of Ramesses II over 19.5 metres high. The one immediately to the left of the entrance was destroyed in antiquity, pre-sumably by an earthquake. To the right and left of each colossus and between their legs are smaller statues of other members of the royal family. The façade is crowned by a cavetto cornice, above which is a row of baboons worshipping the rising sun. This photograph was taken prior to the removal of the temple to higher ground.

61 Four Osirid statues of Ramesses II within the Great Temple at Abu Simbel. The statues, over 9 metres high, line the north side of the main axis of the hypostyle hall and stand in front of four square pillars supporting the roof. There are four similar statues on the south side of the hall. The hypostyle hall is the first and largest of a series of chambers penetrating 55 metres into the cliff. They lead to a small sanctuary containing large seated statues of Ptah, Amon, Re-Horakhte, and Ra-messes II.

62 The little Temple at Abu Simbel, dedi-cated to the goddess Hathor. View from the west bank of the Nile looking west. This temple is located a short distance north of the Great Temple and has a rock-hewn façade 28 metres long and 12 metres high. On either side of the entrance are two large standing statues of Ramesses II flanking a third statue of his principal wife, Nefertari. All of these statues wear elaborate crowns. The statues are separated by buttress-like projections. The interior chambers of the temple penetrate over 21 metres into the cliff.

63 Relief inside the Hathor Temple portray-
ing Queen Nefertari being crowned by the
goddesses Hathor and Isis. It is located to
the right of the entrance on the west wall of
the transverse chamber in front of the
sanctuary.

64 Temple of Ramesses II at Wadi es-Sebua.
View southeast from rear of temple towards the Nile, showing sand-filled court
and stone pylon in front of which stood
four large statues of the king. Two fore-
courts and the temple precinct were surrounded by mud brick walls now largely
disappeared. The temple was dedicated to
Amon, Re-Horakhte, and Ramesses. Its
hypostyle hall and sanctuary were cut from
the living rock. Height of pylon 20 metres,
width 24.4 metres.

65 The only column still standing of the
temple at Sedeinga. This temple, located a
short distance north of Soleb, was constructed by Amenhotep III and dedicated
to the cult of his wife Tiy, who appears to
have been worshipped with her husband
as a patron divinity of the region. The
capital of the column was appropriately
decorated with representations of the head
of the goddess Hathor.

66 Temple of Amenhotep III at Soleb. View
of columns in the first court of the temple,
looking northeast towards the pylon. The
papyriform columns resemble those erected
around the court of Amenhotep III's
temple at Luxor. Soleb has been described
as the finest Egyptian temple in Nubia. Its
ancient name was Khaemmat, 'Shining in
Truth'. The temple was dedicated to the
cult of the deified Amenhotep III and of
Amon.

67 One of a pair of monumental red granite
lions originally in the avenue of approach
to the temple of Soleb. Begun by Amenhotep III, this statue was completed and
inscribed by Tutankhamen. Both lions
were removed to Gebel Barkal by the kings
of the Twenty-fifth Dynasty. Length 2.15
metres. British Museum.

68 Two shawabtis, of grey-green serpentine,
mummiform, with plain wig and beard.
Both have incised crossed hands and are
inscribed with a shawabti text and the title
and name 'Prince of Miam, Hekanefer'.
They were found in the fill near the bottom
of the pit leading to the burial chambers in
the tomb of Hekanefer at Toshka East.
Although both are broken, the workmanship is very fine and suggests they were
made in Thebes, the Egyptian capital.
Height of left figure, 20.5 cm.

69 Decoration of west wall of tomb of Pennut
at Aniba. In the upper register the deceased
and his wife are pictured being led before
Osiris by the god Horus. Pennut was
Deputy of Wawat under Ramesses VI and
the inscriptions in his tomb provide important information about the administration
of Lower Nubia during the Twentieth
Dynasty.

70 Garrison quarters against the north wall of
the fortress of Dorginarti. View looking
west. The ruins of a stone glacis can be seen
beyond the water-eroded west (upstream)
tip of the fort. Although this was the lowest
preserved level in the interior of the fort,
pottery, small finds, and inscriptions indicate a late New Kingdom date for its
(final?) occupation.

71 Gebel Barkal, with the great temple of Amon (B 500) at its base. Founded in the New Kingdom the temple was repaired and extended by Piye and other Twenty-fifth Dynasty monarchs. Gebel Barkal is a sandstone butte 93 metres high and was revered by the Egyptians and Kushites as a Holy Mountain. It has been suggested that the face of Gebel Barkal was adorned with four colossal figures of Taharqa, cut from the rock after the style of Abu Simbel. Other scholars believe these 'statues' to be natural formations. The view is looking west.

72 The royal cemetery at Kurru prior to excavation between 1916 and 1919. The view is looking northwest from the ruins of Kurru I, a post Twenty-fifth Dynasty pyramid. The low mounds in the middle distance are mastabas belonging to the 'main row'. Beyond is the low knoll that is the highest point in the cemetery. It contained the earliest tumuli burials (*c.* 850 BC).

73 Broken but almost complete statue of King Taharqa in a striding pose. Of black granite. Found at Gebel Barkal. The king is portrayed in typical Pharaonic style. He wears a tight-fitting cap adorned with two uraei and surmounted by tall plumes. The rough finish of this crown was probably to facilitate gilding. The tight cap is typical of monarchs of the Twenty-fifth Dynasty. The statue is inscribed down the back and on the belt. Merowe Museum No. 11; Khartoum 1841. Total height *c.* 4.18 metres.

74 Great Temple of Amon (B 500) at Gebel Barkal. Looking east from the top of the hill. The outer court (being excavated by Reisner in this photograph) was the work of Piye, while the inner court, nearer the hill, was part of the original New Kingdom temple, but contained a kiosk of Tanwetamani. The inner part of the temple, at the foot of Gebel Barkal, was a mixture of New Kingdom constructions, with additions and repairs of the Twenty-fifth Dynasty and later.

Index

Index

Index

DATE DUE

JAN 0 3 2006			
B1105-11 DUE 12/05/07 Due 01/02/08			